IRISH STUDIES
1

EDITED BY P. J. DRUDY
FELLOW OF ST EDMUND'S HOUSE, CAMBRIDGE

CAMBRIDGE UNIVERSITY PRESS

LONDON   NEW YORK   NEW ROCHELLE
MELBOURNE   SYDNEY

Published by the Press Syndicate of the University of Cambridge
The Pitt Building, Trumpington Street, Cambridge CB2 IRP
32 East 57th Street, New York, NY 10022, USA
296 Beaconsfield Parade, Middle Park, Melbourne 3206, Australia

First published 1980

Text set in 11/13 pt Linotron 202 Bembo, printed and
bound in Great Britain at The Pitman Press, Bath

British Library Cataloguing in Publication Data
Irish studies.
    1. Ireland – Civilization.
    I. Drudy, P J
    941.5   DA925   80-40084
    ISBN 0 521 23336 4

Contents

v

Editor's preface

This is the first volume of an interdisciplinary Irish Studies series to be published by Cambridge University Press under my editorship. The aim of the series is to bring together the work of the best scholars currently working on Ireland and on Ireland's relationship with the wider world. Ireland and the Irish are probably best known for their literature – the works of Yeats, Joyce, and Beckett, for example, are required reading for most university literature courses. Unfortunately, much important historical work on Ireland is less well known. Similarly, research in the economic, social, political, and more general cultural spheres has tended to be published within Ireland, mainly for an Irish readership. This series will attempt to redress the balance, and, by appealing to an international audience, to reduce those misunderstandings about Ireland that may still remain. It is my view that a deeper understanding can be best achieved in the context of a wide range of scholarship over a wide range of disciplines.

In view of Ireland's literary tradition it seemed appropriate that this first volume should concentrate on literature. However, it also includes a number of important contributions from historians. Some chapters break new ground; others cast a refreshing new look on already-trodden territory. The volume is mainly concerned with the nineteenth and twentieth centuries.

Future volumes will focus around specific titles and, though by no means ignoring literature, will place more emphasis on economic, social, and political matters. Volume 2 will be entitled *Ireland: people, politics and the land* and will be published in 1981.

My sincere thanks are due to my advisory editors for their advice and assistance. I am similarly deeply indebted to the Syndics of Cambridge University Press, and to Dr Andrew Brown who planned the series with me. Dennis Forbes, Maureen Leach, James Butler and John Gray of the Press also provided much moral and technical support. Lastly, I wish to thank my wife, Sheelagh, who encouraged my efforts and helped in many ways. I am grateful to all of them.

P.J.D.

St Edmund's House,
Cambridge
October 1979

A tale of two islands: reflections on the Irish Literary Revival

SÉAMUS HEANEY

In the summer of 1892, Sir Charles Gavan Duffy returned to Ireland after a distinguished political career in Australia. Fifty years earlier he had been closely identified with the Young Ireland Movement, with the patriot Thomas Davis and with that most influential of Irish nineteenth-century journals, *The Nation*. It was in the pages of *The Nation* in the early 1840s that the potent connection between Irish writing, Irish history and anti-Union politics was securely forged, a connection which Dr Conor Cruise O'Brien would see as 'a dangerous intersection' – dangerous to civic order in the thinking of the mature O'Brien, and dangerous to literature in the thinking of the young W. B. Yeats.[1] Nevertheless, Yeats had invited Gavan Duffy to Dublin.

The old journalist patriot was being wooed by the young poet visionary because there was a special post to be filled within the newly formed Irish Literary Society, and Yeats was taking the hint that John O'Leary gave him when O'Leary said, 'In this country a man must have upon his side the Church or the Fenians, and you will never have the Church.' With Gavan Duffy involved, the Irish Literary Society would be sure of popular support, although Yeats did have his reluctances which quickly turned into opposition to that much travelled patriot.

That opposition arose in the course of setting up a scheme for an Irish Library to be published by Fisher Unwin and Company in London. Both men had notions of an Ireland renewed through the influence of books, but one sentence of Gavan Duffy's will suffice to show how their notions were bound to be at variance. 'Good books', Duffy declared, 'make us wiser, manlier, more honest and what is less than

I

any of these, more prosperous.'[2] The utilitarian soul that lay
behind such sentiments could never please the romantic poet,
whose vision of Ireland was at this time magical and legendary, and not at all in sympathy with the kind of economic
realism that made Duffy's mind tick and his pen deliver
sentences like the following, one of my favourite declarations
by an Irish writer. 'When I met in France, Italy and Egypt the
marmalade manufactured at Dundee, I felt it as a silent
reproach.'[3]

It may have been a memory of that marmalade that
provided Yeats with his exact and demeaning image of
orange-peel, when he came to remember Duffy years later in
his *Autobiographies*.

One imagined his youth in some gaunt little Irish town, where no
building or custom is revered for its antiquity; and there speaking a
language where no word, even in solitude, is ever spoken slowly
and carefully because of emotional implication; and of his manhood
in practical politics, of the dirty piece of orange-peel in the corner
of the stairs as one climbs up to some newspaper office; of public
meetings where it would be treacherous amid so much geniality to
speak or even think of anything that might cause a moment's
misunderstanding in one's own party.[4]

Gavan Duffy, in other words, was representative of the
philistine middle classes, who hunted in packs, thought in
slogans and survived in a milieu that was at least vulgar when
it was not vicious; and was, of course, almost certain to be
Catholic. Duffy, Yeats says, was friendly with 'many who at
that time found it difficult to refuse if anybody offered for
sale a pepper-pot shaped to suggest a round tower with a
wolf-dog at its feet, (and) who would have felt it inappro-
priate to publish an Irish book that had not harp and
shamrock and green cover'.[5]

This is the mature Yeats speaking, almost thirty years after
the event, when he was acknowledged master of the Irish
Literary Movement that he is remembering, and the attitudes
about art and Ireland implicit here are the ones which he
enforced upon his disciples and readers and, for that matter,
upon his posterity. They are therefore worth reflecting on.

If we look at those things about Duffy which draw Yeats's contempt, we shall very quickly get a sense of what was likely to earn his respect. There was, first of all, the 'geniality' of those public meetings – the word is dealt out like a flesh wound – a geniality anathema to Yeats, yet in the midst of it we might expect to find the likes of Simon Dedalus, boozy, voluble and political; in such gatherings 'the clever man who cries/the catch cries of the town' was likely to carry the day, and nothing could be expected except 'the beating down of the wise/and great art beaten down'.[6] Over against all this democratic buzz and huddle there stood the patrician figure of the artist, whose solitude and dignity linked him to all that was enduring and pure in the country, to the aristocracy on the one hand, who had made beautiful manners, and to the peasantry, who had made beautiful stories. Far from being genial, he was cold and passionate, an aspect of the betrayed Parnell or the martyred Synge or the equestrian Robert Gregory. This heroic isolation might eventually lead him to the winding stair of an old stone tower, but it would never take him up the stairs of a newspaper office. Instead of orange-peel there would be a stare's nest at the window; instead of living among the detritus of the filthy modern tide, this ideal artist/Irishman would find himself by nature and by right haunting a territory between the ditch-back where the beggar sang and the walled demesne where the patron conducted her salon; or perhaps, if he were shy, he would find himself, like J. M. Synge, lying with his innately pure ear to a crack in the loft floor, registering the speech coming up from the country kitchen underneath, a speech fully flavoured as a nut or an apple, spoken only 'where the springtime of the local life has [not] been forgotten . . . and the straw has [not] been turned into bricks'.[7]

Duffy was disqualified from all this by that 'gaunt little Irish town' which was so architecturally and linguistically deprived as to be a symbol of all that was unremembering, moblike, quotidian, at enmity with imagination. It is true that Yeats and Lady Gregory and J. M. Synge strove to express a vision of Ireland that would alter for the better the destiny of Ireland, but it is also true that they seem to have assented to the Wildean paradox that nothing that actually occurs is of the slightest importance. They were intent on setting a faith in symbol against any sociological exploration, setting myth against history, ecstasy against irony, art against life. Their forward publicity for the Irish Literary Theatre, soon afterwards to become the Abbey Theatre, makes this abundantly clear. Yeats wrote in the Dublin edition of *The Daily Express*:

Victor Hugo has said that in the theatre the mob become a people, and, though this could be perfectly true only of ancient times when the theatre was a part of the ceremonial of religion, I have some hope that if we go on from year to year, we may hope to bring a little ideal into the common thought of our times. The writers, on whom we principally depend, have laboured to be citizens not merely of that passing and modern Ireland of prosaic cynicism and prosaic rivalries, which it may be their duty to condemn, but of that eternal and ancient Ireland which has lived from old times in tender and heroic tales . . . And they have laboured to write of Irish and all other things as men should write who have never doubted that all things are shadows of spiritual things, and that men may come to the gates of peace by beautiful and august thoughts.[8]

Here Yeats is doing in prose what he had already done in verse, defining an Irish reality by flirting with but skirting politics, and giving us that adaptation of the nineteenth-century patriotic tradition which he expressed in his poem 'To Ireland in the Coming Times'. There we find Yeats's brisk tetrameters have somehow disinfected the political content of Davis and muffled the nationalist pulse of Mangan. For it was indeed the spirit of the Unionist, Sir Samuel Ferguson, who moved most influentially through the mind of the young poet, because it was in Ferguson's handling of legendary material that Yeats perceived, consciously or unconsciously, a way of maintaining fidelity to the political and cultural postures of his own class, the middle-class Protestant establishment. At the same time he staked a claim in the very roots of the nationalist Catholic ethos by annexing to himself those native myths and legends and treating them as a unifying rather than a divisive factor. In his *Autobiographies* he gives us an image of Ireland after the death of Parnell being like soft wax, ready to be pressed into a shape determined by the writers, and in articles, poems and speeches Yeats kept striking the shape he wished to conjure. From beginning to end, it is this arrogant but not improper declaration, this *fiat*, which makes him the powerful figure, artistically and culturally, that he is. The definitive poems are full of imperatives and peremptory claims:

> Know, that I would accounted be
> True brother of a company
> That sang, to sweeten Ireland's wrong,
> Ballad and story, *rann* and song.[9]

> You that would judge me, do not judge alone
> This book or that, come to this hallowed place
> Where my friends' portraits hang and look thereon;
> Ireland's history in their lineaments trace;
> Think where man's glory most begins and ends
> And say my glory was I had such friends.[10]

The lineaments in question here, of course, are those of Lady Gregory and John Synge, and it is a special version of history we are asked to trace in those particular faces, and in the faces of Major Robert Gregory and his cousin Sir Hugh Lane – a history where the profiles of noble and beggarman almost blot out the milling background of church and bourgeoisie. These names figure in the Yeats pantheon of 'all the Olympians', related to one another in their aristocratic disdain for onion-sellers and their nonchalant love of excellence, united by various superb analogies and elisions in the course of Yeats's writings with the Dukes of Urbino, Jonathan Swift, Burke, Berkeley and Goldsmith. But in the two opening stanzas of the poem some figures appear who, while they cannot be called friends, do earn their place because they have sufficient intensity of personality or commitment to distinguish them from the orange-peel and oratory of those beyond the circle. There is Roger Casement upon trial, 'half hidden by the bars, / Guarded; Griffith staring in hysterical pride . . . Kevin O'Higgins . . . a soul incapable of remorse or rest'. Yet in that presentation of Griffith, the Sinn Féiner, we

can surely sense more dementia than *sprezzatura*, and in
Kevin O'Higgins, the assassinated Minister for Justice in the
first Free State Government, there is surely a hint of in-
temperance and 'the heart grown brutal' lurking in his 'soul
incapable of remorse or rest'. These figures may be all right
as neighbours to the Olympians on the walls of the Municipal Gallery, but would they want their Olympian daughters to
marry one of them? I think not. Yet it is their un-Olympian
names that are in the history books and their faces keep
looking out to remind us that in ignoring the Ireland of
prosaic rivalries Yeats created a magnificent and persuasive
Ireland of the mind, but a partial one.

So I want to continue with a tale of two islands which will
also yield up a tale of two Irelands, and will eventually lead us
from the Literary Revival towards more recent Irish poetry.

One of the most convincing pieces of evidence for Yeats's
claim that his Abbey writers will deal with the ancient and
permanent Ireland of the spirit comes in J. M. Synge's
account of an island wake and funeral in his book, *The Aran
Islands*, a work of great purity where Synge's style is so
obedient to its matter that it makes even the plangencies of
Riders to the Sea sound as if they are too self-consciously in
pursuit of *duende*:

After Mass this morning an old woman was buried. She lived in the
cottage next mine, and more than once before noon I heard a faint
echo of the keen. I did not go to the wake for fear my presence
might jar upon the mourners, but all last evening I could hear the
strokes of a hammer in the yard, where, in the middle of a little
crowd of idlers, the next of kin laboured slowly at the coffin.
To-day, before the hour of the funeral, poteen was served to a
number of men who stood about upon the road, and a portion was
brought to me in my room. Then the coffin was carried out sewn
loosely in sailcloth, and held near the ground by three cross-poles
lashed upon the top. As we moved down to the low eastern portion
of the island, nearly all the men, and all the oldest women, wearing
petticoats over their heads, came out and joined in the procession.
While the grave was being opened the women sat down among
the flat tombstones, bordered with a pale fringe of early bracken,
and began the wild keen, or crying for the dead. Each old woman,
as she took her turn in the leading recitative, seemed possessed for

the moment with a profound ecstasy of grief, swaying to and fro, and bending her forehead to the stone before her, while she called out to the dead with a perpetually recurring chant of sobs.

All round the graveyard other wrinkled women, looking out from under the deep red petticoats that cloaked them, rocked themselves with the same rhythm, and intoned the inarticulate chant that is sustained by all as an accompaniment.

The morning had been beautifully fine, but as they lowered the coffin into the grave, thunder rumbled overhead and hailstones hissed among the braken.

In Inishmaan one is forced to believe in a sympathy between man and nature, and at this moment when the thunder sounded a death-peal of extraordinary grandeur above the voices of the women, I could see the faces near me stiff and drawn with emotion.

When the coffin was in the grave, and the thunder had rolled away across the hills of Clare, the keen broke out again more passionately than before.

This grief of the keen is no personal complaint for the death of one woman over eighty years, but seems to contain the whole passionate rage that lurks somewhere in every native of the island. In this cry of pain the inner consciousness of the people seems to lay itself bare for an instant, and to reveal the mood of beings who feel their isolation in the face of a universe that wars on them with winds and seas. They are usually silent, but in the presence of death all outward show of indifference or patience is forgotten, and they shriek with pitiable despair before the horror of the fate to which they all are doomed.

Before they covered the coffin an old man kneeled down by the grave and repeated a simple prayer for the dead.

There was an irony in these words of atonement and Catholic belief spoken by voices that were still hoarse with the cries of pagan desperation.

A little beyond the grave I saw a line of old women who had recited in the keen sitting in the shadow of a wall beside the roofless shell of the church. They were still sobbing and shaken with grief, yet they were beginning to talk again of the daily trifles that veil from them the terror of the world.

When we had all come out of the graveyard, and two men had rebuilt the hole in the wall through which the coffin had been carried in, we walked back to the village, talking of anything, and joking of anything, as if merely coming from the boat-slip, or the pier.[11]

This is as much revelation as observation. Undoubtedly, the Aran community is far from the world of editors' offices,

lending libraries and Royal Irish Constabulary police barracks. It has a biblical or Homeric feel to it, and we have only
to imagine that other Dubliner, Oscar Wilde, arriving at the
graveyard, to sense how fundamentally different this life was
from the life of what Synge called 'the coteries'. Yet Synge
and Yeats both began their literary life among the tapestries,
in earshot of 'les sanglots longs/des violons' of Verlaine and
decadence; Arthur Symons dedicated *The Symbolist Movement in Literature* to Yeats, and Synge himself, when Yeats
met him in Paris, was luxuriating in the decadent mode,
writing stuff with titles like 'Etude Morbide' and 'Under
Ether'. Synge had not then discovered that art in order to be
human might have to learn to be brutal. He had not found his
subject, but Yeats was soon to introduce him to it, and when
he died to identify him with it forever, with that 'race |
passionate and simple like his heart'.

Yet the coteries and the Aran people had this much in
common: they were remote from the world of telegrams and
anger, from party splits in Committee Room 13 and from
ivy-days in other Committee Rooms, from sectarianism and
petty Nationalism. Here Home Rule did not matter, nor
Rome Rule. Here was the true source, before 'merchant and
clerk/breathed on the world their timid breath'. What is so
irresistible about the Aran world is its sense of form and
ritual. That sailcloth which carries the coffin, the hammer
blows of the coffin-maker, those red petticoats among the
rocks, the very elements of this life are impeccably aesthetic,
and when the essence of the life expresses itself in the keen,
that expression is again unforgettably dramatic and ritual-
ized. At that moment, there was no need for Synge to feel
that he was a member of the Established Church intruding
upon a congregation of Roman Catholics: these incidental
and slightly vulgar distinctions are consumed and abraded as
Synge and the keening women perne in the gyre of race and
whirl in the vortex of inner consciousness out of the ebb and
flow of the modern tide. And so, what was actual on the
island could become exemplary for and in a literature: the
passion and control, the ferocity and comprehension, the

violence and formality. Just as the discovery of seemingly paradisal cultures in the South Seas and on the American plains enabled the first Romantics in their beliefs in human perfectability, so these last Romantics chose for theme:

> Traditional sanctity and loveliness;
> Whatever's written in what poets name
> The book of the people.[12]

These Anglo-Irish counter-cultural Romantics found in the west of Ireland corroboration for their image of an Ireland untouched by geniality, inoculated against mere opinions and unified by an instinctive sense of beauty.

All this, of course, was artistically proper and exhilarating. Writers need images and situations which release in them whatever is latent and submerged and allow them to appease their perhaps unconscious yearnings and tensions. One has a sense that for Synge there was enormous exultation and confirmation and destination in the Aran experience: he had found a power-point, he was grafted to a tree that had roots touching the rock bottom, he had put on the armour of authentic pre-Christian vision which was a salvation from the fallen world of Unionism and Nationalism, Catholicism and Protestantism, Anglo and Irish, Celtic and Saxon – all those bedevilling abstractions and circumstances. Admittedly, Nationalist Catholic Ireland would wince and whinge at his presentation of western womanhood in *The Playboy of the Western World*, but that was ignorance and prejudice pattering weakly as rain on the strong tegument of his integrity. That was stock reaction by the round-tower and shamrock crowd. Synge rested secure in his sense of having penetrated the real Gaelic soul, of having translated into a work of art in the English language the fundamental attitudes and structures of feeling that he discerned in the Irish language culture of the west. And Synge's achievement was buttressed by the subsequent appearance in Irish and English of an indigenous western literature, notably works by natives of the Blasket Islands such as Tomas O'Criomtháin, Maurice O'Sullivan and Peig Sayers, whose autobiographies confirmed an image

of the native stock as tragic, noble, simple, stoical, poetic.
And Synge's certitude transfused Yeats also, who turned in
scorn from Dublin to the west and to his own dream
fisherman – who at other times may have been a hard-riding
country gentleman – 'climbing up to a place / where stone is
dark under froth'. Thus the actuality of western island life
and western 'big house' culture was given a symbolic resonance that still vibrates and carries.

Yet, as I have said, this actuality was a part of the whole. I
wish to turn now to another island, in the north-west of the
country, on Lough Derg in County Donegal. This is Station
Island or St Patrick's Purgatory where bus-loads of fasting
pilgrims still arrive each summer and where an unbroken
tradition of penitential devotion has existed for centuries.
Famous throughout Europe in the Middle Ages, notorious
during the penal days, it has always been an important
element in Irish Catholic sub-culture. It was to make this
pilgrimage or station that the young William Carleton set out
at the age of nineteen or twenty, in the second decade of the
nineteenth century and it was to this memory he returned
when he began his literary career in the pages of *The Christian
Examiner* in 1828 with the publication of his first work, 'The
Lough Derg Pilgrim', an exercise which launched Carleton
into the composition of one of the most important Irish prose
works of the nineteenth century, his *Traits and Stories of the
Irish Peasantry*. The Lough Derg pilgrim arrives fasting,
continues praying around the stony penitential beds and
spends his first night on the island half awake in relentless
repetition of *paters* and *aves*. Nowadays there is a basilica
where most of this first night is spent, but in Carleton's time
the amenities were not so adequate nor was the nomenclature
so grandiloquent. The site of the overnight devotion was
then known as the 'prison':

On entering the prison, I was struck with the dim religious twilight
of the place. Two candles gleamed faintly from the altar, and there
was something, I thought, of a deadly light about them as they
burned feebly and stilly against the darkness which hung over the
other part of the building. Two priests, facing the congregation,

stood upon the altar, in silence, with pale, spectral visages, their eyes catching an unearthly glare from the sepulchral light of the slender tapers. But that which was strangest of all, and, as I said before, without a parallel in this world, was the impression and effect produced by the deep, drowsy, hollow, hoarse, guttural, ceaseless, and monotonous hum which proceeded from about four hundred individuals half asleep and at prayer; for their cadences were blended and slurred into each other as they repeated, in an awe-struck and earnest undertone, the prayers in which they were engaged. It was certainly the strangest sound I ever heard, and resembled a thousand subterraneous groans, uttered in a kind of low, deep, unvaried chant. Nothing could produce a sense of gloomy alarm in a weak superstitious mind equal to this; and it derived much of its wild and singular character, as well as of its lethargic influence, from its continuity; for it still – still rung lowly and supernaturally on my ear. Perhaps the deep, wavy prolongation of the bass of a large cathedral bell, or that low, continuous sound which is distinct from its higher and louder intonations, would give a faint notion of it – yet only a faint one; for the body of hoarse monotony here was immense. Indeed, such a noise has something so powerfully lulling, that human nature, even excited by the terrible suggestions of superstitious fear, was scarcely able to withstand it.[13]

The style of this is by no means as chaste as the style of Synge, yet the subject itself, the sound that a world makes, invites us to compare and meditate. For just as Synge found in the uncontaminated bravery of the keen a register to which he could tune his own sensibility, that separate sensibility of the Anglo-Irish, so Carleton's country Catholic being responds in complete harmony to the humbled melodies of his own patient debilitated tribe. Yeats would eventually annex Carleton into his network of forbears of the Celtic Twilight and try to escape the tedious actualities and impoverishments of the century which Carleton lived and wrote by calling him 'the greatest novelist of Ireland by right of the most Celtic eyes that ever gazed from under the brow of storyteller'.[14] But it is not the fabled Celtic quality which is significant about Carleton. Rather, it is the marks he bears in his sensibility and watermarks into his writing of experiences not archetypal but historical, not ennobling but disabling.

Synge studied Irish at Trinity College, Carleton learned his
Latin at a hedge school; Synge reworked the locutions of
Wicklow vagrants while residing at vicarages and castles in
the neighbourhood, Carleton saw the gibbeted bodies of
Ribbonmen hanging by the roads of County Louth while he
hunted for a post as a hedge-schoolmaster. Synge's artistic
ambitions led him to a Parisian hotel room from which he
was rescued by a great poet, Carleton's financial desperation
led him up the perhaps orange-peel strewn stairs of an office
to write anti-Papist propaganda for the Reverend Caesar
Otway. Synge's discovery of his subject involved an escape,
Carleton's involved a denial.

Carleton became a member of the Established Church and
wrote at first to corroborate the attitudes of 'that lean
controversialist', Otway. In 'The Lough Derg Pilgrim', for
example, the word 'superstition' clamours for a hearing and
occurs twice in the passage just quoted. But what remains
most potently in the mind is the substance of what is being
condemned: the music of that underworld which made
Carleton was the music of his own humanity. His will did
not work hard enough to subdue his imagination, and so we
have that strange weltering world of the *Traits and Stories*,
written from within the circle, by a man whose ears and
nostrils were full of the intimacies and exactitudes of poverty. His world, instead of being described and idealized from
without – Synge, for example, is shy of entering the wake-
house – is welling up from within himself. His English does
not consciously seek for Irish effects but has only recently
emerged from the Irish language itself and if it has a less
perfect finish than Synge's, it embodies what Synge admired
in peasant speech – hyperbole, ebullience and range of intonation.

Carleton wrote copiously, politically, imperfectly. He
became embroiled in the politics of O'Connell and of Young
Ireland, he wrote on landlordism as well as on superstition,
he flailed between the attitudes of his adopted faith and the
affection of his deserted tribe, but he wrote without any
sacral sense of the race he belonged to, a figure of con-

troversy because of his apostasy but a witness to a realistic, politicized Ireland that the nineteenth-century poets and their revival heirs could not or would not voice. Consider, for example, what Yeats makes of the Lough Derg pilgrim. This poem, included in his *Last Poems*, by no means represents Yeats at his best but it does have enough that is typical of his note and attitude to underline a point in this context:

THE PILGRIM

I fasted for some forty days on bread and buttermilk,
For passing round the bottle with girls in rags or silk,
In country shawl or Paris cloak, had put my wits astray,
And what's the good of women, for all that they can say
Is fol de rol de rolly O.

Round Lough Derg's holy island I went upon the stones,
I prayed at all the Stations upon my marrow-bones,
And there I found an old man, and though I prayed all day
And that old man beside me, nothing would he say
But fol de rol de rolly O.

All know that all the dead in the world about that place are stuck,
And that should mother seek her son she'd have but little luck
Because the fires of Purgatory have ate their shapes away;
I swear to God I questioned them, and all they had to say
Was fol de rol de rolly O.

A great black ragged bird appeared when I was in the boat;
Some twenty feet from tip to tip had it stretched rightly out,
With flopping and with flapping it made a great display,
But I never stopped to question, what could the boatman say
But fol de rol de rolly O.

Now I am in the public-house and lean upon the wall,
So come in rags or come in silk, in cloak or country shawl,
And come with learned lovers or with what men you may,
For I can put the whole lot down, and all I have to say
Is fol de rol de rolly O.[15]

That is the pilgrim as hard-riding country gentleman, more a case of indomitable Irishry than penitential action. It was Patrick Kavanagh who coined the word that describes this note: 'buckleppin', a kind of bollocky, histrionic hop and skip that is finally another case of will doing the work of imagination. And imagine if Yeats had got away with it.

Imagine if we had to take these images as exemplary, in the way we were instructed to:

> Sing the peasantry, and then
> Hard riding country gentlemen,
> The holiness of monks, and after
> Porter drinkers' randy laughter.[16]

Austin Clarke was obedient to the directive for the first half of his career. He turned to Fenian lore for his early epic tales, and then the holiness of monks and the randiness not only of porter drinkers but of monks and maidens in the medieval period became his theme. Next, most appositely for our purpose, he published in 1929 a volume called *Pilgrimage*, full of grey water and bare thorn, fire and ice; a book in which the cold weather of a wintry Irish landscape and the illuminated glow of Celtic manuscripts combined to render an imaginative world at once meagre and familiar, rich and strange. But Clarke was to burst through this vestment of Celtic monasticism and break into a much more subjective confessional poetry of self-inquisition in which the perennial flesh/spirit dichotomy within the Irish Catholic mind appeared not as a racial attribute but as a personal cry. From being a frieze of symbolic figures representative of the matter of Ireland, Clarke's poetry become a series of rapid probes and sketches which were symptomatic of what was the matter with Ireland. The shade of the confessional, a shade that never darkened the mind of any character in Yeats or Synge, lies upon Clarke's later work and the power of middle-class Victorian Catholicism begins to be felt in twentieth-century Irish verse. Again, a whole spiritual world for which the revival writers could never have found the proper language begins to emerge into Irish poetry and continues to find its deepened, darkened expression in the work of Thomas Kinsella, the major voice of the generation following Clarke and Kavanagh.

Patrick Kavanagh was born in Inniskeen in County Monaghan in 1905, the son of a cobbler, and he lived the life of a small farmer in his own territory until he was in his early thirties when, like Carleton a century before, his literary talent brought him to Dublin. 'My childhood', he declared, 'was the normal barbaric life of the Irish country poor',[17] and his longest and strongest poem is an anatomy of that life. 'The Great Hunger', published in 1942, is a presentation of rural life denuded of all beautiful folk elements. Among other things, it is a powerful rebuke to the Ascendancy myth of the peasantry, full of love for the hard actualities of small farm life in south-west Ulster but also full of anger against its deprivations, sexual, cultural and spiritual.

Instead of mythologizing the race, Kavanagh anatomized the parish. His sensibility was closer to Carleton's than to Yeats's or Synge's. This was a case of the peasantry not wanting to be sung, but wanting to sing themselves, and finding themselves faced with a version of their own reality that would have to be dismantled. The vehemence of much of Kavanagh's criticism and the air of exhaustion which finally enters his poetry springs, in large measure, from the sway which the Yeatsian image of the country and country people had gained. It was as if he had been imaginatively checkmated: the roots of his poetic gift were deeply entwined in the earth of rural Irish life with all its peculiar hardness and tenderness, yet he began to feel that to call upon those roots and to conjure with those authentic images was somehow to connive in a spurious myth. Hence the barefaced and abrupt absolutes he comes out with from the late forties onwards:

I would say now that the so-called Irish Literary movement which purported to be so frightfully Irish and racy of the Celtic soil was a thoroughgoing English-bred lie.[18]

When I came to Dublin the Irish Literary affair was booming. It was the notion that Dublin was a literary metropolis and Ireland, as invented and patented by Yeats, Lady Gregory and Synge, a spiritual entity.[19]

The Irish audience that I came into contact with tried to draw out of me everything that was loud, journalistic and untrue. Such as:

> My soul was an old horse
> Offered for sale in twenty fairs.

Anthologists everywhere keep asking for this . . . What the alleged poetry-lover loved was the Irishness of the thing. Irishness is a form of anti-art. A way of posing as a poet without actually being one. [20]

Kavanagh elaborates this last insight cruelly but comically in an essay on Yeats's protégé, F. R. Higgins, a man from the rich farmlands of County Meath who wrote a kind of crepuscular Leinster pastoral, a mode calculated to exacerbate the later Kavanagh:

He wanted to be what mystically, or poetically, does not exist, an 'Irishman'. He wanted to be a droll, gallivanting 'Irishman'. Nearly everything about Higgins would need to be put into inverted commas . . . The word 'gallivanting' appears throughout his verse. [21]

Such Irishness, Kavanagh claimed, was not so much a symptom of achieved identity and cultural integrity as it was a symptom of 'provincialism', and as an alternative to such an insincere basis for art, he offered the notion of 'parochialism':

Parochialism and provincialism are opposites. The provincial has no mind of his own: he does not trust what his eyes see until he has heard what the metropolis – towards which his eyes are turned – has to say . . . The parochial mentality, on the other hand, is never in any doubt about the social and artistic validity of his parish. All great civilizations are based on the parish – Greek, Israelite, English. [22]

So Kavanagh's 'Epic', the poem which most succinctly defines his theme and his matter, does not deal with the matter of Ireland but the matter of Inniskeen, not with *arms and the man* in any national sense but with pitchforks and neighbours, with an act of trespass rather than an act of war:

EPIC

I have lived in important places, times
When great events were decided, who owned
That half a rood of rock, a no-man's land
Surrounded by our pitchfork-armed claims.
I heard the Duffys shouting 'Damn your soul'
And old McCabe stripped to the waist, seen
Step the plot defying blue cast-steel –
'Here is the march along these iron stones'

That was the year of the Munich bother. Which
Was more important? I inclined
To lose my faith in Ballyrush and Gortin
Till Homer's ghost came whispering to my mind
He said: I made the Iliad from such
A local row. Gods make their own importance.[23]

Kavanagh brought us forward from the myths of the revival, certainly, but in order to begin again he had to return us to the matter of Carleton.

The great and true liberator was, of course, Joyce who, like Tiresias, foresuffered all. In one well-known and central diary entry at the end of *A Portrait of the Artist as a Young Man*, the whole problem of the Irish artist and his inheritance is vividly exposed:

14 April: John Alphonsus Mulrennan has just returned from the west of Ireland. (European and Asiatic papers please copy.) He told us he met an old man there in a mountain cabin. Old man had red eyes and short pipe.
Old man spoke Irish. Mulrennan spoke Irish. Then old man and Mulrennan spoke English. Mulrennan spoke to him about the universe and stars. Old man sat, listened, smoked, spat. Then said:

– Ah, there must be terrible queer creatures at the latter end of the world.
I fear him. I fear his redrimmed horny eyes. It is with him I must struggle all through this night till day come, till he or I lie dead, gripping him by the sinewy throat till . . . Till what? Till he yield to me? No. I mean no harm.[24]

The old man represents the claims of the pious archetype on the free spirit. Stephen fears him because his red-rimmed horny eyes are in the end myopic, because that mountain cabin where he lodges is hung with the nets of nationality, religion, family, the arresting abstractions. Yet Stephen will not destroy him. The old man is as much a victim as the writer. His illiterate fidelities are the object of Stephen's scepticism, the substance of what Stephen rejects; and yet they are a part of Stephen himself. Stephen is angry that all his culture can offer him for veneration is this peasant oracle, yet understanding the ruination that he and the old man share, he is not prepared to struggle to the death.

Yeats's stance, and Lady Gregory' and Synge's towards the old man are very different. He is for them a portal, a gleam of half-extinguished thought. They would give him artificial respiration whereas Stephen's impulse is to strangle him. For Stephen has suddenly come to rely on the self, on the resources of his intellect, on the facts of his personal life and learning. A sudden thrust of confidence in the validity of his own enterprise liberates him. From being on the defensive, he is suddenly on the offensive.

Joyce did not seek to use myths to establish a racial separateness or a national literature. He was not immediately interested in a coherent Irish tradition but was necessarily content to inherit the shattered one which history bequeathed him. Stephen tells Davin, the young Gaelic League enthusiast, that he is not prepared to pay in his life and person for the mistakes which his people have made. Instead, he will forge a personal truth. He will use myth not to construct exemplary alternative worlds but to structure the facts of his own bourgeois Catholic experience. We will have the Hades chapter of *Ulysses* instead of the Aran keen, we will have the aeolus chapter to redeem the orange-peel.

And it is surely the Joycean example that was at the back of Thomas Kinsella's mind when he doubted whether a coherent national literary tradition was necessarily an advantage, and went on to declare that every modern writer inherits a gapped and polyglot tradition anyhow. Kinsella, another Dubliner, has learned from Joyce and from others beyond Ireland, as we all must learn, ways of including within the house of poetry life that has heretofore shivered in the gaunt towns and the superstitious minds. Eliot, and Jung, and Dante enable him as well. I shall end with an extract from his recent elegy for his father, a poem which he published separately in a red cover, with a design resembling exactly the design of a pious Catholic magazine called *The Messenger*, which is also the title of Kinsella's poem. But where the Jesuits print on their red cover an image of the Sacred Heart of Jesus, Kinsella has Mercury, a messenger of a different sort. Where they have decorated their cover with the papal keys and emblems of the power of the *ecclesia*, Kinsella has the label of a Guinness bottle, since his father worked for that firm, and the plough and the stars, the device of the labour movement, since the father founded the first trade union in Guinness's. In the extract, the triumph of the child/father is not unrelated to the triumph of the artist/son: both of them are faring forward, carrying the energy of a submerged milieu into a new and affirmative manifestation:

> Deeper. The room where they all lived
> behind the shop. It is dark here too – shut off
> by the narrow yard. But it doesn't matter:
>
> It is bustling with pleasure.
> A new messenger boy
> stands there in uniform, with shining belt!
>
> He is all excitement: arms akimbo,
> A thumb crooked by the telegram pouch,
> shoes polished, and a way to make in the world.
>
> His eyes are bright,
> his schoolmaster's tags fresh in mind.
> He has a few of the Gentlemen's Sixpenny Library
>
> under the bed – *A Midsummer Night's Dream*,
> *Sartor Resartus, The Divine Comedy*, with a notebook,
> Moore's *Melodies*, a trifle shaken . . . Shelley, unbound . . .
>
> He unprops the great post office bicycle
> from the sewing-machine and wheels it through the passage
> by odours of apron and cabbage-water and whitewashed damp
>
> through the shop and into the street.
> It faces uphill. The urchin mounts. I see
> a flash of pedals! And a clean pair of heels![25]

Philip Larkin has written that 'what will survive of us is love' and has called that 'an almost instinct, almost true'. My almost instinct was that much that had been known and loved in Ireland was half-frustrated in its expression by the mighty beauties of the art of the Irish Literary Revival. What I have been saying here is at least almost true, and if not the whole truth, then let it be taken, itself, as a near myth.

1. S. Deane, 'Literary Myths of the Revival: A Case for their Abandonment', in Joseph Ronsley (ed.), *Myth and Reality in*

Irish Literature (Waterloo, 1977), pp. 317–19. I am indebted to Dr Deane, not only for this article, but for many conversations in which we plied the substance of what I have written here.

2. Quoted by Malcolm Brown in *Politics of Irish Literature* (London, 1972), p. 357.

3. *Ibid.*, p. 357.

4. W. B. Yeats, *Autobiographies* (London, 1956), p. 225.

5. *Ibid.*, p. 203.

6. W. B. Yeats, 'The Fisherman' in *Collected Poems* (London, 1961), pp. 166–7.

7. J. M. Synge, *The Dramatic Works of J. M. Synge* (Dublin, 1915), p. 185.

8. W. B. Yeats, *Uncollected Prose*, vol. 2, ed. by John P. Frayne (London, 1975).

9. Yeats, 'To Ireland in the Coming Times' in *Collected Poems*, p. 56.

10. Yeats, 'The Municipal Gallery Revisited' in *Collected Poems*, p. 370.

11. J. M. Synge, *Four Plays and the Aran Islands* (London, 1962), pp. 190–2. See also Sean Ó Tuama's discussion of this passage in Maurice Harmon (ed.), *J. M. Synge: Centenary Papers* (Dublin, 1972), pp. 1–17.

12. Yeats, 'Coole Park and Ballylee, 1931' in *Collected Poems*, p. 276.

13. William Carleton, *Wildgoose Lodge and Other Stories* (Cork, 1973), p. 109.

14. William Carleton, *Stories from Carleton* with an introduction by W. B. Yeats (London, 1889).

15. Yeats, *Collected Poems,* pp. 360–1.

16. Yeats, 'Under Benbulben' in *Collected Poems*, p. 400.

17. Patrick Kavanagh, *Collected Pruse* (London, 1967), p. 14.

18. *Ibid.*, p. 13.

19. *Ibid.*, pp. 14–15.

20. *Ibid.*, p. 16.

21. Patrick Kavanagh, *November Haggard* edited by Peter Kavanagh (New York, 1971), p. 19.

22. *Collected Pruse*, p. 282.

23. Patrick Kavanagh, *Collected Poems* (London, 1972), p. 136.

24. James Joyce, *A Portrait of the Artist as a Young Man* (Harmondsworth, 1960), pp. 251–2. See also Thomas Flanagan, *The Irish Novelists, 1800–1850* (New York, 1959), pp. 333–40.

25. Thomas Kinsella, *The Messenger* (Dublin, 1978), p. 18.

Church, state and Irish Christianity

DAVID FORD

The relationship of church to state is one of the most fascinating themes in western history. It sounds through the Roman Empire into the Middle Ages, Renaissance and Reformation, and then into the modern era of nation states and the French, American and Russian revolutions. It is the story of the meeting of two claims, each in some sense absolute, and of the resulting tensions, conflicts and *modi vivendi*, in which issues of the most fundamental importance for civilization have been focused. It has been a massively complex interaction stimulating thought and action in politics, law, ethics and religion, and has been a major constant factor in the evolution of patterns of power-sharing, rights and liberties.

The central point at issue has been the competence of the state in matters of religion. There has been a wide variety of solutions to this. Often the church's policy has changed according to its political power, as seen in Augustine's *volte face* in relation to the Donatists (and his fateful principle that error has no rights), and the similar changes of Luther, Melanchthon and Calvin as their movements attained more secular power. The intervening medieval period could be seen as a long struggle to settle the spheres of church and empire, with important and lasting institutional and cultural effects. But as the European nation states emerged the tension tended to be resolved in an Erastian way, with the state in varying degrees dominating the national church. The Reformation continued and at first intensified this trend, and there followed an era of confessional states. There arose conflicting absolute religious claims at the same time as the claims of states became increasingly similar, autonomous and confident. Into this situation, with its many unsatisfactory and contradictory elements, came two events archetypal for modern church–state relations.

The first was the American Revolution. The American Constitution, as worked out in the years after 1787, proposed a new form of church–state relationship. The wording of the First Amendment is: 'Congress shall make no law respecting an establishment of religion, or prohibiting the free exercise thereof'. This negative limitation on the power of the state enabled the USA to break out of many vicious circles, and, to many people's surprise, led to a situation in which religion flourished. Many factors happily came together to make this solution. There were powerful arguments from persecuted groups such as Baptists and Quakers that religious freedom of this sort was more Christian; there was the influence of John Locke, and the strange combination of the individualist, independent Christianity of the Great Awakening with a similarly-minded deism and rationalism; and there were many circumstances and events – the English Act of Toleration of 1689, the multiplicity of sects, the large number of Americans who belonged to no church, the rise of commerce, the unifying effect of the War of Independence, and the remarkable revolution in Virginia, where within ten years one of the most rigid of establishments became a model of separation of church and state.

The second archetypal event was the French Revolution, which is an instructive contrast to the American. In France, after the failure to revolutionize the church by the Civil Constitution of the Clergy, from 1793 there was an active policy of dechristianization. This continued until Napoleon's Concordat of 1801, but that was by no means the end of the church's troubles. The French experience, together with the wide-spread anti-clerical and anti-Christian results of the French Revolution, was especially traumatic for the Roman Catholic Church. In the nineteenth century it consistently opposed democracy and liberalism, in church–state relations as elsewhere, the two most categorical denunciations of the new developments coming in Pope Gregory XVI's *Mirari*

Vos of 1832 and in Pope Pius IX's *Quanta Cura* of 1864 with its 'Syllabus of Errors'. Throughout, there was an acute recognition of the danger of atheist, totalitarian states, but the only alternative was seen as a return to the old autocratic confessional state.

The French attempt to dictate to the church in positive terms, and the accompanying assumption of all authority by the state, contrasts with the American limitation to negatives. The Americans (admittedly in a very different situation) had shown a liberal way that was benevolent towards religion. However, this was not appreciated by the Roman Catholic Church. The experience of Daniel O'Connell in Ireland was also largely ignored. He attempted to mobilize a people without a violent revolution, and to unite Christianity and the struggle for liberalization. It took over a hundred years for the position to change, and then there occurred one of the most staggering reversals in the history of Roman Catholic teaching.

In 1963 Pope John XXIII's Encyclical *Pacem in Terris*, and, two years later, Vatican II's 'Declaration on Religious Freedom', made a *volte face* in relation to *Mirari Vos* and *Quanta Cura*. The American bishops at Vatican II played an important role in passing the Declaration, and the substance was deeply in harmony with their own first amendment. The new position was essentially one of the separation of church and state, though by no means ruling out less liberal solutions than the American. The ideal was now that of religious liberty within a constitutional state. The state is no longer seen as guardian of the religious truth, but rather of the theological freedom of all its citizens, and this not in a spirit of reluctant tolerance but one of active support for religious freedom. All of this is set in a context of recognition of a new situation, especially as regards the importance of human dignity and rights and the accompanying political aspirations and movements.

This epochal shift is an appropriate point to pass to the more particular focus of this chapter, the Irish situation. How does it connect with the history briefly outlined above? The

events that have most deeply determined it took place in the
post-Reformation era of confessional states. That is when
Henry VIII broke with Rome and asserted royal supremacy
over the Church of England; when in Ireland, after an initial
period of moderate persuasion, by the time of Elizabeth I
there was a change towards a policy of plantation and
religious coercion.[1] This was the time of the first successes of
the Counter–Reformation in Ireland and of the missed
opportunity of the Protestant Church of Ireland to establish
itself as the church of the mass of the Irish people. It is
probable that the roots of modern Irish nationalism can be
traced back to this period. Similarly many of the deepest
characteristics of Irish Presbyterianism can be seen in the
double aspect of a Calvinist theology which confirmed the
settlers' self-understanding as a separate, favoured community, and a 'revival' impulse seen for the first time in the
seventeenth century – the first 'awakening' in Irish Protestantism took place under the influence of Calvinist evangel-
ists who took a hard line against Roman Catholicism.

The subsequent history of colonialism, a minority church
established by law until 1869, the continued clash of cultures,
and the tribal hostility and violence is not my business in this
short chapter, but it is vital to note that the main patterns
were laid down in that time of confessional states. They
received their most recent injection of new life in the
nineteenth century. On the Protestant side there was a major
revival which partly reinforced the mainstream churches, but
also produced many smaller, intense groups, among them
the direct ancestors of the Reverend Ian Paisley's church. On
the Catholic side there was an even more complete devotional revolution, in which Daniel O'Connell's movements
played their part, and which identified later largely with the
Home Rule movement. This Catholic revival was, strange to
say, strengthened by the major nineteenth-century Irish
tragedy, the Great Famine. The class which formed the
backbone of the new-style church of Cardinal Cullen, the
tenant farmers with more than thirty acres, and those in the
towns of comparable standing, emerged more numerous and

wealthy from the disaster, and were able to provide the large number of priests and nuns, as well as the finance, for the church, educational and welfare organizations that were set up.[2] The strategy of Cardinal Cullen and his fellow bishops in education was particularly important. Their successful political stance of both being in favour of Home Rule and also bargaining with the British government for immediate concessions, resulted in their gaining control of an educational network which they could retain after independence and partition.[3] The control was not merely clerical, it was strongly episcopal, and this is still a factor in the Irish situation.

In all, there took place in the nineteenth century a close interweaving of Catholic and Irish identity. The tradition of Wolfe Tone and the rise of Sinn Féin did not have much effect on this. Such events as the virtual concordat of the Irish Catholic bishops with Parnell in 1886, and, in the twentieth century, recognition of common interests by the hierarchy and de Valera on a wide range of issues, have determined the course of Irish politics more than have either the Anglo-Irish cultural contribution or the cases of opposition by republicans to Catholic church authority. On the Protestant side a religio-political unity was also being strengthened in the nineteenth century, especially as Home Rule became imminent, and so the eventual solution of partition should not seem surprising. It is clear that the main impulse towards this came from the Protestant side, but the solution was probably not unwelcome either to the Catholic bishops or to many national politicians. For the former the attraction of a 90 per cent Catholic state in the south was greater than that of a united Ireland with a substantial anti-clerical minority. As regards the national politicians, their political bases were not in the north-east, and its inclusion might well have upset the balance of power in the new state, even if this had been possible without civil war.[4]

In the years since the partition of Ireland in 1921 the main lines of the nineteenth-century divisions have not changed. Indeed, the policies of governments on both sides did a great deal to reinforce them, with results that are obvious today. There are a number of 'old chestnuts' which symbolize the problem of the past sixty years. The central one is that of the political unity of the island. The contemporary form of this dilemma is simply stated:

Just as the Northern minority will never peacefully tolerate a restoration of the Stormont regime, so the Northern majority will never peacefully enter the Republic.[5]

Irishmen and others can test their prejudice by asking themselves which side of that they generally understress. The conclusion is clear:

If Ireland is to be united, then the Republic and Northern Ireland must both alike disappear and be replaced by some radically different structure. It is impossible to prescribe in detail the pattern of such a structure, but two things are clear: it would have to be based on some system of community rights; and the traditional concept of majority rule would have to be abandoned.[6]

The other old chestnuts relate to this in various ways. In the Republic there are the role of the Irish language, the legal position on contraception, divorce and abortion, and the complex field of education.[7] In the north there is also the education issue,[8] and there are segregation, discrimination and the problem of law, order and violence.[9] In both too, there is the question of mixed Catholic–Protestant marriages, in relation to which an Irish Theological Association working party described the present Roman Catholic regulations as one of the most divisive religious features in the present situation in Ireland.[10]

Yet a 'no change' verdict on the situation would be a great mistake. The sense of change in Ireland is indeed such that many people feel that they are already well into a new era, although it is not yet clear what its main features are. There are the obvious elements of accelerated industrialization and urbanization, the growth of mass culture, with its 'mid-Atlantic' ethos, and the new turn given to these processes both by the membership of the whole island in the European Economic Community and by the growing crisis symbolized by the energy situation. One would expect these to have the effect on the churches that sociologists (using varying definitions) call 'secularization', the retreat of religion from public to private life and an increasing difficulty in seeing its relevance or meaning in relation to the whole of life. This is certainly partly true of Ireland, especially many younger people (who now make up a disproportionately large percentage of the population), but there has as yet been no dramatic break with the past. Will there be? The question as to whether the divisions of the island can be healed without a major catastrophe and further bloodshed is perhaps the most fundamental question that can be asked on the subject of this chapter. Is time running out for the churches, and are developments building up to their widespread dismissal and rejection?

Here we are faced with the inadequacy of formulating the problem as one of church and state. A better way is to see both church and state as factors influencing and being influenced by Irish society.[11] This does not ignore the importance of the constitutional and legal issues mentioned above, but it does emphasize the deeper processes which determine such formal decisions, and so helps to focus energy on the long-term quality of Irish society and Christianity.

On an international level it is not only economic and social factors that have brought great changes, but also those in world Christianity. The dramatic reversal of Roman Catholic teaching on church, state and religious freedom has already been mentioned. This means that in contrast with other countries which faced comparable situations before Vatican II, and in contrast with Ireland in previous crises, Ireland today has the great advantage of official Catholic support for a realistically pluralist solution. Irish history and religion have not encouraged the growth of that liberal, tolerant frame of mind expressed in the American Constitution, but now at the world level the Roman Catholic Church has disavowed its own teaching of the nineteenth century, the very time when the present Irish divisions received the

stamp that they still carry. This is not the only aspect of
Vatican II to have deep importance for traditional Irish
positions: its encouragement of lay ministry, power-sharing
by bishops with clergy and laity, ecumenism, a new style and
content in social teaching, a freshly Christ-centred understanding of the church, energetic biblical study, and dialogue
and co-operation of many sorts together forms a most
appropriate agenda for Ireland. Indeed, as signs of reacting
against, or simply ignoring it, multiply, a decisive question for
the rising generation of Irish Catholics is how far they will be
guided by the light of Vatican II.

On the Protestant side there have also been great changes
internationally.[12] It is no accident that the Reverend Ian
Paisley is so hostile to ecumenism, to the WCC and to
modern scholarship, since they represent developments (pre-
dating and conditioning Vatican II) that have drastic implications for his position, and for the whole political and
religious ecology of Northern Ireland. But how much effect
have such factors had on mainstream Irish Protestantism?
There is a mixed overall picture and young Protestants are
faced with at least as fundamental questions as young Catholics. I will remark on just two further areas of importance to
both parties.

The first is that of praise and worship. Perhaps the most
dramatic thing that has happened between the mainstream
churches in recent decades has been joint participation in
prayer and praise. The charismatic movement has deservedly
been the main focus of comment, though that comment has
often been superficial. In fact the movement makes sound
sense at every level. Sociologically, there is a great need in the
modern church for groups that fill the gap between the
individual (or the small family) and the whole parish, since
modern society has been most destructive of these intermedi-
ate groupings. It is also perhaps true that only in such a
medium-sized group can one find the personal contact with
those of varied experiences and ages, frank sharing and
conversation, security, encouragement and informal accul-
turation that are so necessary to sustain and develop a pattern

of life which many elements in the culture tend to discourage. So, psychologically and educationally (or catechetically) these groups meet a need which few natural families have the resources to meet. In simple Christian terms such groups are places where the process of thoroughgoing conversion is likely to be facilitated, and from the ecumenical standpoint there is probably no better way for Christians to grow together on a specifically Christian basis than to do something that all churches acknowledge as of the highest importance. And theologically, it is not surprising that a concentration above all on praising and loving God should have beneficial effects on all the other levels as well.

The charismatic is only one of many contemporary movements, Christian and others, that rely primarily upon such 'basic groups'. Their problems and possibilities are a lively area of discussion, but in the churches they generally seem to pose problems of life and growth (often of something like adolescence) rather than, as so often, of decline and death. The lesson in Ireland seems to be this: that already such groups have had a significant impact north and south, and that they could well be a key factor in the sort of devotional revolution that corresponds to the needs and opportunities of the twentieth century.[13] As I said above, the previous such revolutions have reinforced denominational and political divisions, but the world situation and that in Ireland have now made possible a spirituality that, with other factors at other levels, could transform the picture presented in this article.

The second area of common concern to the churches in Ireland that I want to discuss is more general. The disaster of Irish Christianity is that a religion with reconciliation as its *raison d'être* is a major factor in dividing a country. The one aspect of this that I choose to focus on now is the role of a community's 'overarching story', or (in its more technical but still, I feel, misleading sense) 'myth', in shaping and maintaining its identity and its habits of thought and action. The story of Jesus's life, climaxed in his death and resurrection, and understood by Christians as harking back to creation and forward to the consummation of world history, is such a story for all Christians. In Irish Christianity the dominant overarching story for each community has been strongly distorted to serve the ends of a competitive super-iority. The stubbornness with which each story is main-tained, in subtle and crude ways, and the assimilation of all new evidence to it, is a commonplace of Irish life, and is as true of the south as the north. It amounts to a web of intermingled truth and falsehood in which each side's story has enough truth to render it plausible, although the outside world's verdict on them may change (and there is a major propaganda battle waged to affect this verdict). All media are used in serving each story, the most abhorred forms of betrayal consist in disloyalty to it, and outsiders who do not have either story in their bones are seen as naive.

Alexander Solzhenitsyn, in his Nobel Prize speech, spoke of the strong connection between lies and violence. Violence may function for a while without much ideological backing, but if it is to establish itself it needs justification, and this involves the systematic corruption of intellect and feeling. In line with this, the theologian Karl Barth saw falsehood as the crowning sin, and most productive of misery. I consider that the chief responsibility of the churches for the violence in Ireland today is to be found in this area. It concerns what is most properly within their direct influence, the spheres of common belief and education. They have promoted or acquiesced in misleading, slanted overarching stories, both their own and each other's. This has been done both positive-ly and negatively, by simply ignoring the other, and also by insufficient concentration on the great overarching story they both share. The men of violence are parasitic on the com-munal identity, fear and perspectives that have resulted, and the recent years of cruelty and murder have simply added new events and incidents to each side's story and reinforced it in a vicious circle.

The mainstream churches have had an incomparably better record in this crisis than in any similar one in the past. Their role in each state has in this century moved generally towards being the conscience of society and away from assumptions of theocracy, or that majority morality must be state law,[14] and this has put them in a far better position to co-operate in responding to the recent phase of violence. Yet they have understandably been slow in the more searching forms of self-examination. The extent to which they need to criticize and revise their overarching stories has become clear, especially to many of those whose education and culture puts their church allegiance at risk. The result is that the possibility of massive defections from all the churches due to lack of credibility (not only in their handling of the Irish question, however, but in their whole response to contemporary reality) is increasing all the time, and it could happen quite suddenly.

Yet there is another side that I have already hinted at, which is made up of the good possibilities in Irish Christianity. Ireland has the advantage of meeting many of its problems after other countries and churches have already tried to deal with similar ones. It also has a faith with deep roots, and enough committed people to make important changes in church life affect the whole country. Also it has, paradoxically, had the benefit of the recent years of crisis, which have mobilized many to Christian action in a way nothing else could (for example, in the Women's Peace Movement), and have provoked individuals and groups into just the sort of self-examination and change that are needed. It does not take long to discover in Ireland today a whole network of hopeful initiatives. But my final example will be one of the stubborn issues, by no means the chief one, but yet illuminating.

It is that of theological education. This century has had a great flowering of theology, Catholic and Protestant, but Ireland has had little part in it. The types of Christianity flourishing in Ireland have mostly been quite anti-intellectual, and a whole level of the church's ecology has therefore been despised and neglected. Anti-intellectualism is a form of falsehood that undermines integrity in the long term, and that leaves a community badly equipped for the

ideological warfare it faces. In Ireland theologians are not
much encouraged, and there are few institutions in which
Protestant and Catholic theologians can work alongside each
other. There has been much more contact and collaboration
in recent years, ranging from the Ballymascanlon ecumenical
meetings to informal visiting lecture arrangements, but there
is a great need for an institutional setting, preferably in the
universities. The attempts to bring this about have symbolized in microcosm many of the dilemmas discussed in this
paper, most especially those concerned with education and
the overarching stories within which people live. At the time
of writing, although there is a new non-denominational
theology course at Trinity College, Dublin, there is still no
interdenominational co-operation in this area. The universities in Cork, Galway and Dublin are forbidden to teach
theology by their constitution and it would need state
legislation to change this. Theology is therefore not allowed
a full relationship with other disciplines, or any part in the
academic atmosphere in which most of the island's students
are educated.

This chapter has been quite general, and very selective in
its examples. In particular the major differences between each
of the mainstream churches have not been elaborated, though
there are references to literature on them. The conclusion is
that, whatever the political solution to the Northern Ireland
situation, Irish Christianity is a focus for a complex of
elements that have already changed its role in relation to state
and society, and that face it now with the greatest task, and
danger, in its history. The evolution of church–state relations
has been from the confessional state type to the benevolent
separation of church and state (further advanced in the north
than in the south), and this has been in line with international
trends in mainstream churches and liberal democracies. The
future policies of governments north and south are unlikely
to have great surprises in this area. The great unknown is the
quality of church initiatives and responses for the rest of the
century, on which much of the distinctiveness of Irish society
depends. It is no exaggeration that there is the possibility of a

new Christian option in modern society if a creative way through is found, yet it is hard to find any vision of this that rings true.[15]

1. See Brendan Bradshaw, 'Sword, Word and Strategy in the Reformation in Ireland', *The Historical Journal*, vol. 21, no. 3, 1978, pp. 475ff.

2. See Emmet Larkin, *The Roman Catholic Church and the Creation of the Modern Irish State: 1878–1886* (Dublin, 1975). Cf. the review of Larkin by David W. Miller in *Irish Historical Studies* vol. 20, no. 78, 1976, pp. 212ff.

3. See David W. Miller, *Church State and Nation in Ireland: 1898–1921* (Dublin 1973).

4. *Ibid.*, especially pp. 485ff.

5. J. C. Beckett, 'Memorandum on Irish Unity', Appendix A in the Church of Ireland *Report of the Role of the Church Committee* (Dublin 1973).

6. *Ibid.*

7. See J. H. Whyte, *Church and State in Modern Ireland 1923–1970* (Dublin, 1971); Michael Hurley, S. J. (ed.), *Irish Anglicanism 1869–1969* (Dublin, 1970).

8. See *ibid.*; Martin Wallace, *Northern Ireland. Fifty Years of Self-Government* (Newton Abbott, 1971).

9. See *Violence in Ireland. A Report to the Churches* (Belfast and Dublin, 1976, 1977).

10. Quoted with comment in a Church of Ireland statement, reported in *The Irish Times*, 19 July 1979.

11. See Enda McDonagh, 'The Believing Community and the Political Community. A New Framework for Church–State Relations', *The Maynooth Review*, vol. 4, no. 2, (1978); cf. *Church and State Opening a new Ecumenical Discussion* (World Council of Churches, Faith and Order Paper, no. 85, Geneva, 1978).

12. *Ibid.*

13. I am grateful to the writings, graduate seminars and conversations of my colleague, Professor Walter Hollenweger, for help in appreciating the phenomenon of the pentecostal and charismatic movements and in particular their political significance. His major work is *The Pentecostals* (London, 1972).

14. See Liam Ryan, 'The Church and Politics', *The Furrow*, vol. 30, no. 1, 1979; Fergal O'Connor, 'Church and State', *The Furrow*, vol. 30, no. 5, 1979; J. H. Whyte, *Church and State*; *The Northern Ireland Situation: 3 Statements by the Presbyterian Church in Ireland, 1968–74* (Belfast, 1974).

15. The first version of this chapter was presented to a meeting of the British–Irish Theological Seminar in September 1978 on the theme 'Reconciliation and Redemption in the 1980s'. I am most grateful for the comments and criticisms received there, and also for help from the Most Rev. Dr G. O. Simms, Dr F. S. L. Lyons, Rev. James Hartin, Dr Garrett Fitzgerald, and my brother Alan Ford.

Frank O'Connor and Gaelic Ireland

RUTH SHERRY

When Frank O'Connor (Michael Francis O'Donovan) was born in 1903, his native Cork was essentially an English-speaking city. There were, however, Irish-speaking pockets in outlying districts in County Cork, and many people who had moved into Cork City from the countryside had Irish as their native language, although their city-born children did not. In the springtime of the Gaelic League, there was often an ironic discontinuity between the sensibilities of Gaelic League adherents who were concerned to preserve Irish and the culture associated with it, and the sensibilities of the urbanized country people who were in the process of losing that language and culture.

In *An Only Child* O'Connor records the history of his early relationship with the Irish language and the Gaelic cultural movement.[1] Irish was first brought to his attention by Daniel Corkery, who taught him for a brief period when he was a small child and became his hero and guide in adolescence. O'Connor's mother, whom he adored, was exclusively English-speaking. His relationship with his father was, even at best, difficult, and he tended to regard his father's family with dislike and resentment, contrasting their slovenliness with his mother's refinement. It was only after he began to learn Irish from Corkery that he realized that his father's mother was a native speaker of Irish. From the beginning Gaelic Ireland thus had conflicting associations for O'Connor; Corkery, like his mother, represented enlightenment to him, while his father's family represented ignorance and degradation.

From Corkery O'Connor took the devotion to the Irish language and its literature which was to stay with him for the

35

rest of his life. By late adolescence he had begun to write in Modern Irish and to translate from the language; in time he taught himself Old and Middle Irish as well. O'Connor also took from Corkery his cultural and political nationalism, but this, as we shall see, was shorter-lived.

O'Connor's efforts to come to peace with both mother and father, his efforts to integrate what he saw as opposed aspects of his heritage, inform much of his writing. Many stories deal more or less explicitly with his relations with his father, and his grandmother served as a model for characters in various works. In *My Father's Son* O'Connor deliberately attempts to present a balanced view of his father to compensate for his youthful rejection of him.[2] The title of *My Father's Son* is however equivocal, for in this autobiographical work O'Connor also describes a number of close relationships with older men who succeeded Corkery as father surrogates. Like Corkery, these men – Yeats, George Russell, Richard Hayes – all had credentials of one kind or another as nationalists or as devotees of Gaelic culture. Yet his relationships with them were not always smooth either, and his later attitudes toward the Irish language, toward Gaelic culture and traditional ways of life, reflect the complexity of his heritage and early experience. His mature position, as this essay attempts to show, was not a simple one and was not untouched by ambivalence.

A complicating factor in O'Connor's attitude toward Gaelic Ireland is its political dimension. During the Civil War O'Connor, who with Sean O'Faolain was still a follower of Corkery, fought on the Republican side and was interned. During the course of his detention, however, he became disillusioned with the cause he had fought for, and especially with its leaders, whom he came to see as committed to cold abstractions and divorced from the human consequences of the decisions they took. In particular he developed what became an enduring contempt for de Valera, who himself might be seen as a father figure for generations of Irishmen.[3] De Valera's attempts to reinstate the Irish language and his tendency to idealize the Gaelic world, past and present, were not to be exempted from attack. It was in the years following the Civil War that O'Connor's relationship with Corkery became strained, largely because O'Connor could no longer accept Corkery's form of nationalism, equally intransigent culturally and politically.

Unlike the extreme nationalists, O'Connor, for all his devotion to the Irish language and its poetry, refused to admire every phenomenon which could be labelled Gaelic. One of the problems he faced in his attitude toward Gaelic Ireland came simply from the fact that it was dying out. Although Irish had once been the language of powerful aristocratic and scholarly classes which gave a high place to poetry, by the end of the nineteenth century it was the language of the most deprived parts of Ireland, the inhabitants living on the edge of subsistence, often illiterate. From such circumstances his grandmother had come. For the son of convent-raised Minnie O'Donovan, who struggled against great odds to maintain a decent life in Cork City, the real world of Gaelic Ireland was an alien one, even though it preserved remnants of the old high culture. To idealize it in de Valera's fashion often seemed to O'Connor like idealizing poverty and ignorance.

O'Connor's concern for the problem of modern Ireland's relation to Gaelic Ireland is one which is reflected in a number of his short stories, especially ones written in the 1930s and the beginning of the 1940s; it was during the earlier part of his career that he was most preoccupied with this problem and its significance for him as a writer. In time he did arrive at his own resolution of the conflicting aspects of the issue. Viewing O'Connor's position in political terms, one can see him as a representative of the first generation of modern Irish writers for whom the British were no longer the essential enemy; the significant conflicts were now to be found within Ireland herself. The stories in which O'Connor explores the relationship between modern Ireland and traditional, rural, Gaelic Ireland are varied, some comic, others sombre. What they have in common is a tendency to define the relationship between the two Irelands as one of opposition. The two worlds generally cannot be integrated, yet for individual characters this opposition is a matter of internal conflict, divided loyalties, unfulfillable aspirations, an opposition leading even to tragedy.

O'Connor's first collection of short stories, *Guests of the Nation*,[4] generally expresses a rather mixed view of its main subject, the Civil War. Some of the stories reflect a youthful love of adventure and sense of vitality, but often they see absurdity or viciousness given licence under the name of patriotism. One story, 'The Patriarch', describes the experience of a Cork child who comes under the influence of a much older 'patriot' (significantly corrupted to 'patriarch' in the lanes of Cork) and grows up to take his mentor's place when the old man becomes too feeble to continue his participation in the struggle.

The opening section of the story satirizes deliciously the kind of ignorant nationalistic enthusiasm which assumes that everything Gaelic is also patriotic and idealistic. The 'Patriarch', a shopkeeper, pure 'townie', offers free sweets to any child who can speak a few words of Irish, a language he himself doesn't know and can't learn. The protagonist, Dermod, eager for the reward, pesters his Irish-speaking grandmother (clearly derived from O'Connor's own grandmother) to teach him a few sentences, but the earthy songs and sayings she produces have no connection with the Patriarch's sentimental dreams.

When he saw me, the Patriarch began to speak in his vivid and moving way about Holy Ireland, and about the beautiful tongue in which our fathers had sent down their message of undying hatred to children forgetful of their fame. . . . I was induced to sing an Irish chorus that I had picked up from my grandmother. The old man listened in an almost ecstasy . . .

I translated literally as I had heard my grandmother do:
'O, my wife and my children and my little spinning-wheel. My couple of pounds of flax each day not spun – two days she's in bed for one she's about the house, and Oh, may the dear God help me to get rid of her!'

'Are you sure you have the meaning right, *a ghile*?' he asked at last.

'That's what my grandmother says,' I replied, feeling the next word would make me weep . . .

'I have it . . . 'Tis England he means. The bad wife in the house. That's it – I have it all straightened out now. You have to have them songs interpreted for you. The pounds of flax she didn't spin are all the industries she ruined on us. England, the bad wife – ah, how true it is. Dark songs for a people in chains.'[5]

The comic and satirical tone of the opening later modulates into a more solemn mood. The story traces Dermod's growth to manhood, where he and his generation act out, in the Troubles, the consequences of the old man's principles. Dermod retains his affection for the Patriarch, but loses his reverence for him as the old man reverts to childishness and dies as fanatically devoted to the obscure St Rita of Cascia as he once was to Dark Rosaleen. As a whole the story outlines the familiar process of disillusionment and growing up away from one's early heroes which O'Connor in his own life experienced in relation to Corkery, who presided over his early patriotic education.

Several stories written in the next few years focus on the conflict between modern and traditional Ireland. In some of these stories the Irish language is not specifically at issue, but the traditional values they are concerned with derive from a culture which was certainly Gaelic. 'Peasants', a story more purely comic than 'The Patriarch', deals with traditionalists who are indifferent to the modern legal system, derived as it is from Roman and English law. They continue to operate with centuries-old, heroic notions of honour, loyalty, and retribution.

When a young man, Michael John Cronin, steals the funds of 'the Carricknabreena Hurling, Football and Temperance Association',[6] the other members are prepared to cope with his action by reminding themselves and everyone else in the village of all his worthless relatives and ancestors generations back. By 'naming' him in this way they reaffirm the stability and continuity of the communal order, which depends, as in all tradition-based communities, upon fixed roles and identities for all members. Michael John is to be punished in the accepted way by a kind of banishment – his relatives collect money to send him to America, and justice will thus be done without reference to any outside authority.

This highly satisfactory solution is thwarted by the parish priest, Father Crowley, a comparative newcomer who sees himself to be in a power struggle with 'the long-tailed families' of the village. He is determined that Michael John must be prosecuted. For the villagers this prospect implies the betrayal of one of their own to outsiders, and involves holding not only Michael John, but all his relatives and indeed the whole village, up to the scorn of the rest of the world. 'The like of this had never been heard of in the parish before. What? Put the police on a boy and he in trouble?'[7]

The comedy of the story depends upon the confrontation of these two unquestioned systems of value, each held with Bergsonian rigidity. Michael John restores the money, thus cancelling the crime according to traditional views; then the villagers propose that, even if Father Crowley feels obliged to turn the boy over to the police, he should later rescue him by 'giving him a character' in court; finally they offer the priest a contribution, like a blood-price, 'to cover the expense and trouble to yourself'.[8] All these stratagems are rejected with increasing vituperation by Father Crowley.

Although the story treats comically the villagers' inability to see beyond their inherited assumptions, in the end the traditional values are vindicated. Michael John must serve a short term in prison, but Father Crowley is soon driven away from Carricknabreena by the hostility of his parishioners. When Michael John emerges from prison, his neighbours feel that he must be recompensed for his trouble. Using this money he sets himself up in business, and, taking on the role of a gombeen man, becomes a curse to the village, a result which is blamed upon the priest. This ironic ending refutes the official legal system's premise that punishment produces reform; the older system of banishing the offender to America at least got him out of the place.

The conflict in 'Peasants' depends upon the situation of an isolated community which has been rooted in one place for centuries. The very title ('peasant' is not a neutral term in Ireland) reflects both the priest's scornful attitude toward the country people and the fact that these families have been tied to one plot of land for generations, a situation in which people *must* live together forever afterward. In such circumstances abstract modes of punishment like brief imprisonment are futile. The only sensible way of dealing with so anti-social an element as Michael John is to get rid of him altogether.

It is perhaps unexpected that a city-born-and-bred writer should show so sympathetic an insight into an essentially rural frame of mind, even though the sympathy is coloured by irony in 'Peasants'. O'Connor's experiences in the Civil War had however brought him into touch with the Irish-speaking country of West Cork, and his later occupation as a librarian in Sligo, Wicklow and Cork often sent him travelling into the countryside in the course of his work.

It made me realize that I was a townie and would never be anything else. In the best of the houses I visited – usually the houses of people who had been prominent in the Troubles – the people were better related to the wild countryside about them than I am to the tame city about me. Seeing them in Cork in their uncouth clothes with their uncouth accents was one thing; seeing them on their own farms was another thing entirely, and it made me conscious of my own uncouthness rather than theirs. But those families were few, and the total effect of the country on me was one of depression.[9]

Despite this ambivalence O'Connor seems to have derived from these experiences a more than conventional sympathy with traditional ways of thinking.

The tenacity of traditional concepts of justice and resistance to modern law in isolated communities is the subject matter of several other stories written at about the same time as 'Peasants'. 'Tears, Idle Tears',[10] a rather inferior piece of work, tells of a village which covers up an accidental death for the benefit of a policeman who might be inclined to view it as a crime. In contrast to 'Peasants', 'Tears, Idle Tears' presents resistance to the law as rather ridiculous. The main point of the story is however the solidarity of the villagers, who retain all possible affection for the sergeant at the same time that they plot to deceive him.

'The Majesty of the Law' is a much finer story, and is one of O'Connor's best-known; also essentially comic, it perhaps gives greater hope for the integration of the traditional and modern worlds than do the other stories considered here. A police sergeant goes to visit Dan, an old man living alone in the hills. At the end of the visit the sergeant reveals for the first time his real purpose in coming. Dan has refused to pay a fine imposed as a result of a quarrel with a neighbour, and willingly agrees to go to prison. Dan is following a strategy which derives from an ancient heroic code of pride and shame. ' "I'll punish him. I'll lie on bare boards for him. I'll suffer for him . . . so that neither he nor any of his children will be able to raise their heads for the shame of it" '.[11] The device of using one's own suffering to shame one's enemy is of course not dead; hunger strikes and many other forms of passive resistance are based on it and have in particular been associated with Irish Republicanism. Yeats roots the strategy in antiquity in 'The King's Threshold', where the sufferer, like Dan, emerges victorious.

Dan is conscious of himself as the survivor of a way of life which is on the verge of extinction. His conversation with the sergeant consists largely of a lament for the loss of old medicines, old ways of making whisky, old songs.

'Every art has its secrets, and the secrets of distilling are being lost the way the old songs were lost. When I was a boy there wasn't a man in the barony but had a hundred songs in his head, but with people running here, there, and everywhere, the songs were lost . . . Men die and men are born, and where one man drained another will plow, but a secret lost is lost forever'.[12]

The sergeant in this story is a figure caught between the two worlds. He is a representative of the alien legal system which forbids the distilling of poteen, but in many ways his sympathies are with the old man rather than with the new system. Most of the story consists in fact of a description of a sensitive and ceremonious exchange of courtesies between the two men, host and guest. The obligations of the traditions of hospitality are accepted by both, to the point that each disowns his convictions out of courtesy; Dan defends the law against illegal distilling and the sergeant proclaims that the law was a mistake.

To the extent that the policeman shares the virtues of hospitality with Dan, he represents a continuation of the old order in the modern world, but if he is to be courteous, he must defy the very laws he represents, drinking on duty and accepting an illegal bottle as a gift. The new order has not succeeded in integrating the old traditions into its institutions, even though they are still respected by individuals. Dan, in the end, is the comic victor who employs the prescriptions of the new law in the service of the old, the title of the story referring directly to Dan's traditional code and ironically to the modern one. But Dan is an old man who has never married, and therefore does not imply any future; the sergeant by contrast has a wife and children (who incidentally 'run here, there, and everywhere') and the ultimate triumph of the new institutions is thereby suggested. Dan is furthermore faintly corrupted; for company he feels he should offer 'two handsomely decorated cups, the only cups he had, which, though chipped and handleless, were used at all only on very rare occasions; for himself he preferred his tea from a basin'.[13] One feels that his basin, and 'the seats of the chairs [which] were only slices of log, rough and round and thick as the saw had left them',[14] are more authentic expressions of the old man's nature than the half-understood cups – yet the desire to give the best to the visitor is pure enough.

'In the Train' treats the traditional moral code much more harshly than the stories previously considered. Helena Maguire is guilty of murder, but her 'peasant' neighbours will not testify against her in the courts, and she is acquitted. They plan, nevertheless, to use their own method of punishing her – 'to give her the hunt' and drive her from her own village as Father Crowley was driven from Carricknabreena. The framework of the story is a journey between the city where the trial was held and the remote village to which murderer, witnesses and policemen are all returning. In the train they are all in a suspended state, relieved of the demands made by the places at the extreme ends of the journey. The policemen are able to share illegal liquor with the villagers, and the villagers are able to chatter with the woman they will reject and drive away, but as the train nears its destination they separate once again into their own parties, police on one side, witnesses on the other, and the murderer left alone and despairing.

During the journey there is much discussion about the relative value of the village, Farranchreest, and the city; in this story modern Ireland is represented most forcefully by the wife of the police sergeant, an unpleasant woman who feels superior to everyone else by virtue of her middle-class town upbringing: ' "I was educated in a convent and play the piano; my father was a literary man and yet I am compelled to associate with the lowest types of humanity." '[15] She is hardly a recommendation for modern Ireland, and yet by contrast with the punishment the murderer will receive, a conviction in the court would seem almost a kindness. The murder itself appears incidental, insignificant by comparison to the larger conflict between what is represented by town and village. If Dan in 'The Majesty of the Law' is one of those perfectly related to the wild countryside around him, 'In the Train' suggests why O'Connor as a young librarian nevertheless found the countryside depressing.

The conflicts between old and new which interest O'Connor are not confined to matters of law and justice. 'In the Train' emphasizes the real power which remains in traditional communities, but in 'The Bridal Night' O'Connor's subject is rather the vulnerability of those still left in remote Irish-speaking districts. This story is probably the finest of those considered here, and the one which offers the most subtle treatment of the problem under discussion. The narrator, a visitor to a lonely Irish-speaking district, meets an old woman who tells him of her one son, Denis, who has been in an asylum in Cork for many years. Denis fell in love with Winnie Regan, a well-off girl from a town who came to the place as a schoolteacher, but the love was a hopeless one and he went mad because of it. Winnie, who did not intend to encourage him, was nevertheless sorry for him and, to calm him, lay beside him the night before he was to be taken away. Although she risked her reputation by doing so, she earned the respect of the local people and became a kind of heroine. The old woman tells the stranger her story, praises Winnie, and mourns for her son.

The story has an ancient, almost Greek, feeling about it in its sense of the inevitability of suffering, especially the suffering of the innocent and helpless. It reflects the classical sense of love as a curse, a form of madness. The old woman, Mrs Sullivan, reflects the traditional representations of Ireland as an old woman, Kathleen ni Houlihan, mourning the loss of her sons; but whereas Kathleen ni Houlihan conventionally mourns sons lost to the British or gone into exile, here the loss is caused by something else, the intrusion of the towns into traditional districts. Winnie is a *stranger* in this place, with a different language, a different education, and, of course, money. The gap between her world and Denis's is so great that Mrs Sullivan is resigned to the impossibility of there being any match between her and Denis.

Winnie is an ambiguous figure in the story. She is the outsider, part of the new native ruling class (that is, the Catholic middle class) which has replaced the Anglo-Irish and the British, but her intentions are beyond reproach. Winnie has learned Irish, even if it is only 'book Irish', and as Mrs Sullivan says, ' "She came here of her own choice, for the great liking she had for the sea and the mountains." '[16] The story acknowledges a strange unity and sympathy which extends from Winnie and her world to that of the Sullivans. Her independence and lack of conventionality, established early in the story by her habit of sitting and reading or writing in the cove in isolation, are the same characteristics which give her the capacity to make her gesture of sympathy with Denis, and she is then in turn accorded the honour of the people of the place.

Yet there is some ambivalence in Mrs Sullivan's account of

her. One cannot blame Winnie for Denis's hopeless passion
and madness, yet everything his mother says reflects her
sense of Denis's goodness and worth; why isn't he good
enough for Winnie? ' "A quiet, good-natured boy and
another would take pity on him, knowing he would make
her a fine steady husband, but she was not the sort, and well I
knew it from the first day I laid eyes on her." '17 Denis's
madness, after all, consists *only* in being a poor country boy
who falls in love with a town girl who has money. The loss
of Denis for the old woman is not only the loss of a son, but of
her whole family, any chance of grandchildren, as expressed
in her remembering the old song, 'Lonely rock is the one
wife my children will know'; by extension, the gradual death
of the Gaeltacht is implicit.

There is thus a tension between acceptance of the situation,
resignation, and a feeling of its inevitability on the one hand;
and a sense of frustration, regret and rebellion on the other.
One might also ask what the effect is of Mrs Sullivan's telling
the story to the stranger, himself presumably a representative
of Winnie's world. 'Town Irish' travel often enough, after
all, to the isolated places – frequently, like their prototype
Synge, with the motive of learning Irish and the way of life
associated with it – but they *are* town people, as O'Connor
acknowledged himself to be. They do not come without
bringing change; they rarely settle and become integrated
into a Gaeltacht community, and they thus inevitably stand
in ambiguous relationship to the culture which they both
value and reject. Mrs Sullivan kisses Winnie's hands as the
people used to kiss the hands of the old aristocrats, and it is
Winnie, with her money, education, mobility and courage,
who has all the potential for action in the situation. Denis and
his mother are merely acted upon.

'Uprooted' treats an experience which have become increasingly common in Ireland – the movement of population
from rural places to towns. A Kerry boy, Ned, has deliberately chosen to leave home, and has achieved his ambition of
becoming a schoolteacher in Dublin. Yet he is vaguely, but
deeply, dissatisfied. He returns for a long weekend to his old

home, in company with his brother Tom who is a priest. The Kerry landscape is described with a colour and vividness not common in O'Connor's stories, which are not usually given to much physical description.

Very little happens by way of plot. Ned and Tom visit friends and relatives; Ned sees the beauty of the countryside with new eyes, and is tempted to remain at home and marry a local girl. But when his brother Tom expresses dissatisfaction with his own life as a priest, and urges Ned to accept the fulfillment that is ready at hand, Ned does not feel able to do so. ' "We made our choice a long time ago. We can't go back on it now." '[18]

The Kerry world to which Ned and Tom return is described in terms of timelessness; even those things which have in fact changed seem as timeless and familiar as the others: 'The only unfamiliar voice, little Brigid's, seemed the most familiar of all'.[19] But Ned has committed himself to a world in which things must and do change. As he says to Tom, ' "I suppose we must only leave it to time. Time settles everything." '[20]

The impulse which first drove Ned away from his home was one connected with his love of books, which were meaningless to his father. The world of Ned's childhood was one of poverty, with no books, learning, or aspiration – essentially a world with some remnants of art, in the old songs still sung, but a world without the life of the mind, even if the life of the heart was satisfied in it. In the conversation at home, all intellectual curiosity is directed to the question of whose car it was that just went up the road. Having perceived these limitations in the place of his birth, Ned cannot return to it, but the visit home seems to show him, for the first time, some of the beauty of what he has lost. The story expresses the general modern experience of longing for older and simpler modes of life, while at the same time recognizing that they are no longer really available to modern people. The conclusion of the story, which presents traditional Ireland at its most appealing, also gives O'Connor's most explicit statement of the relationship between old

Ireland and new Ireland:

> There was a magical light on everything. A boy on a horse rose suddenly against the sky, a startling picture. Through the apple-green light over Carriganassa ran long streaks of crimson, so still they might have been enamelled. Magic, magic, magic! He saw it as in a children's picture-book with all its colours intolerably bright; something he had outgrown and could never return to, while the world he had aspired to was as remote and intangible as it had seemed even in the despair of youth.[21]

Ned's plight is the plight of modern Ireland generally as O'Connor tended to see it: full of aspiration, on the way to something great, but not yet arrived at a state which offered adequate recompense for the irrevocable loss of the old beauties. Significantly, Ned's move to Dublin, like O'Connor's own when he became a librarian in Dublin in 1929, is related to his love of books. In Ned's case, as in O'Connor's own, this love is not appreciated by a father with a great love of the drink. Even in his farewell to Kerry, Ned in his imagination must relate it to a book, though only a child's picture book.[22]

The almost surrealistic use of colour in the passage quoted above may not be merely decorative. O'Connor is not a writer who relies very heavily on symbolism, any more than on visual description. Here, however, one may want to note that the red and green prominent in the ending of the story have appeared earlier, in a description of Ned's life in Dublin, where 'along the edge of the canal . . . the trees become green again and the tall claret-coloured houses are painted on the quiet surface of the water'.[23] The pairing of red and green is of course often associated with Ireland, and was fixed in this significance for literary purposes by Joyce. Perhaps by using them here O'Connor is suggesting that both Dublin and the Kerry Coast are, equally, aspects of Ireland and the Irish experience, however much the gap between the two worlds leads to difficulty for individuals and even whole communities.

'The Long Road to Ummera' insists on the need for respect for the old ways, even from those who find them irrelevant for modern town life, and illustrates the power the old ways may have even over those who would prefer to ignore them. The story is also O'Connor's apology to the grandmother he rejected as a child. The main character, Abby, a snuff-taking, porter-drinking shawlie, is clearly modelled on her. Although she appears to be a negligible figure in her life in Cork City, Abby takes on heroic proportions in the tenacity of her devotion to her dead husband and the countryside she was forced to leave when he died.

Abby tries to extract from her son Pat, a comfortable Cork businessman, a promise that he will take her back to Ummera for her burial, along the same road she took with him when they left. Pat tries to dismiss her memories of dead people and a dead life as insignificant in modern Cork, but when she makes her own arrangements to be taken home to Ummera and dies on the way, Pat is forced to bow to the superior strength of her conviction, and takes her the rest of the road himself. When Pat mocks her interest in the dead, Abby retorts, ' "Isn't there more of us there than here?" '24 Her conviction of the existence of 'us', dead or alive, conveys a sense of human unity and solidarity lacking in Pat's middle-class Cork world.

Abby's belief in the continuing reality of the dead is dramatized by her speaking the phrases of traditional Irish poetry when she is convinced her dead husband has come to lead her away:

'Ah, Michael Driscoll, my friend, my kind comrade, you didn't forget me after all the long years . . . They tried to keep me away, to make me stop among foreigners in the town, but where would I be without you and all the old friends? Stay for me, my treasure, stop and show me the way . . . Be easy now, my brightness, my own kind loving comrade . . . After all the long years I'm on the road to you at last.'25

Although Abby has to go to extremes to elicit respect for her convictions from her son, she finds a natural sympathy in the old women around her in the hospital where she dies and in the Irish-speaking priest who reassures her when she is ill.

She is thus seen as representing a world which, if dying, is not yet dead, one which still can exact tribute from the modern town dweller, rising to magnificence in its eloquence.

'The Old Faith', a slight but amusing story, describes how a bishop and a group of priests, under the influence of a confiscated bottle of poteen, begin exchanging stories about the fairies.[26] To the horror of the one cosmopolitan sceptic in the group, they appear to give the tales full credence. Although the story is wholly comic, O'Connor is clearly on the side of the 'old believers' rather than that of the modern sceptic, and he associates 'the old faith' with a richer and warmer humanity than that represented by the more orthodox priest.

Taken together, these stories demonstrate that O'Connor saw Gaelic Ireland as still a significant element in modern Ireland, one with more moral force than may be immediately apparent. Although a few stories emphasize negative aspects of this heritage, most of them treat it and those who hold it with respect, even love. But the ultimate survival of Gaelic Ireland is nowhere assumed by these stories. However strongly some of them appeal for understanding of the Gaelic world, in other pieces of writing at about the same time O'Connor drew clear boundaries to the extent of his commitment to Gaelic Ireland.

The language question has been a persistent one in independent Ireland. O'Connor for his part consistently opposed the language policies of de Valera's government, no less than its other policies, although sometimes his opposition may appear inconsistent. On the one hand he felt that de Valera's attempts to preserve Irish were in fact likely to ensure that it died out; on the other he was convinced that too much attention to the Irish language and the Gaelic heritage prevented Ireland from making the necessary progress toward becoming a modern nation. Both aspects of his position were clearly articulated in an article, 'Two Languages', published in 1934.

O'Connor believed that by its attempt to keep the Irish

people uncontaminated by all outside influences, the government had ensured that Irish became totally irrelevant to modern life. Attempts to preserve sport, music, dance, even law from any foreign influence were linked to the language revival but helped to discredit it.

The words which change the destiny of the world are still being spoken, and Gaeldom still obstinately refuses to pronounce them . . . The result has been that in spite of government subsidy, Irish has tended to go backward instead of forward, and is at least in as bad a plight now as it was thirty years ago. It is a language quite a number of people understand, a beautiful language eminently suited to the purposes of literature, but no one seems to have the least desire to use it except those with nothing to say.[27]

A sore point was that although the government professed to be eager to subsidize the publication of new work in Irish, it would not in fact support such serious writers as Sean O'Faolain, Peadar O'Donnell and Liam O'Flaherty because their works did not accept the limits of the official moral vision.

The comfortable income [offered by the government to a writer in Irish] . . . is still waiting for someone. But before he claims it, it is as well that he should know the conditions. He must make a denial of the nature of fallen man . . . He must believe that the Irish language is more important than the evolving democracy that gave it back to us, and shut his eyes to all the problems that face his people – to disease, vice, ignorance and poverty. He must never mention infidelity or divorce, or birth control or communism . . . nor may he attack private property or native institutions, or suggest that Irishmen are anything but angels.[28]

The rather surprising conclusion O'Connor drew from these observations was not that the government should arrive at more balanced and effective language policies, but that Irish should be allowed to die.

I should like to see it decided now, once and for all, whether Irish or English is to survive. Bilingualism is not an alternative, and is possible at all only in a country which has no mind to make up. We must choose Irish or English, and if Irish, we must choose a new soul to match it.[29]

O'Connor does not seem to have changed his mind on this

point. Gaelic Ireland in fact ceased to be an important source
of inspiration for his fiction in the early 1940s, yet the
problem of the national heritage continued to preoccupy him
in various other ways for the rest of his life. He continued his
campaign against de Valera's policies (not only language
policies) in journalistic writing, especially in a series of
articles written for the *Sunday Independent* from 1943 to 1945.
By this point O'Connor had suffered the fate of many other
writers and found some of his work banned by the official
censors, for reasons which appear incredible today. The
articles in the *Sunday Independent* were therefore published
under another pseudonym, Ben Mayo,[30] and O'Connor's
authorship of them remained a carefully guarded secret until
after his death.[31]

In these articles, as in others written later, O'Connor
continually insisted that Ireland must have an eye for the
future. He saw Ireland as he saw Ned Keating in
'Uprooted' – inevitably going somewhere new, but still full
of unresolved problems. O'Connor considered that de Valera
and his party used up the energy and resources of the country
in meaningless, often harmful campaigns, preferring to cry
out against the Border and against 'obscene' literature rather
than face real problems of housing, health and education. At
his most incensed O'Connor implied that de Valera had no
genuine programme and relied on emotional devices to stay
in power, picturing Ireland as culturally unique, a bastion of
piety and purity which had to be defended against continual
cultural and moral assaults from outside. Maintaining such a
siege atmosphere would distract from any dissatisfaction at
home. The attempt to impose an ersatz Gaelic culture,
tailored to the official morality, O'Connor saw as part of the
same picture.

Several of the articles in the Ben Mayo series take up the
problem of the language as a major or minor topic, almost
invariably seeing it in terms of de Valera's policies, and
attacking such devices as the Irish language qualification for
government jobs, even medical posts where professional
expertise was desperately needed. In another article in the

same series, however, O'Connor speaks of the Irish language in very positive terms:

The true reasons why we all ought to learn and speak Irish is [sic] that it is bound up with our history, that it is a lovely, if difficult language, and that it contains enshrined in it a wealth of song and story, the loss of which to us and our children would be irreparable . . . If today there is perhaps more Irish but less enthusiasm, may not the cause be that Irish has been divorced from liberty and poetry, music and song, and associated over much with compulsion and with mathematics?[32]

Taken together, the statements of the thirties and forties suggest a man pulled in two directions, trying to find a small safe spot on which to take an individual stance, cherishing Irish but also needing a liberal and cosmopolitan atmosphere in which to flourish, and fearing that the two may be incompatible.

The controversy over *The Tailor and Ansty* highlights O'Connor's dilemma; this book, recording entirely authentic material from the Gaeltacht, was banned as obscene by a government which claimed to have the preservation of Gaelic tradition as one of its major goals. O'Connor's defence of the Tailor merged with his crusade against censorship and de Valera's policies generally, although for obvious reasons he did not take the matter up under the Ben Mayo by-line. In a memorial written at the time of the Tailor's death, O'Connor said, 'This, for me, was his greatest quality – he was a great interpreter of Gaelic Ireland.'[33] Yet a few years later, contemplating the forces which had made the last days of the Tailor and his wife Ansty sad ones, he wrote 'It would be far better that the language and traditions of Ireland should go into the grave with that great-hearted couple than that we should surrender our children to the professors and priests and folklorists.'[34]

Although the matter of the language is a significant and recurrent one in the Ben Mayo articles, in retrospect it may seem that their importance, in terms of O'Connor's concern for Ireland's heritage, lies in a different field altogether. It was here that he first took up his defence of Ireland's national monuments and attacked the neglect of this architectural heritage. The very first article in the Ben Mayo series, 'Irish Ruins Shocked Visitors',[35] sets the keynote for his treatment of this subject, one which he continued to write about until the end of his life. In 1964 he again contributed a series of articles to the *Sunday Independent*, this time as Frank O'Connor, focusing on the glories and neglect of Irish architecture; the content of the latest articles on the subject is virtually indistinguishable from what he wrote more than twenty years earlier.[36] Concern for the neglected monuments, and for interesting domestic architecture as well, forms the greater part of a generally light-hearted book, *Irish Miles*,[37] published in 1947 and based on O'Connor's experiences cycling around Ireland during the Second World War. Much of the same material is taken up again in the longer and more systematic travel book, *Leinster, Munster and Connaught*, published in 1950.

O'Connor's concern for the preservation of the architectural heritage was not confined to buildings such as medieval monasteries which are naturally associated with Gaelic Ireland, but the medieval monuments were the ones almost certain to be in a state of neglect and decay, and it was these which elicited his most passionate defence; early monastic sites were his special concern.

Reading O'Connor's writing on the subject at some distance in time, one is struck by the accuracy of his prophecies: many of the monuments have become even more ruined in the intervening years. Yet one is also conscious that certain of the most important sites, such as Holy Cross Abbey, have in fact since been given the careful attention and preservation he was pleading for. Although many voices have been raised in defence of these treasures, O'Connor's was certainly one of the most significant, and he must be given some credit for the practical effects of his campaign.

The last aspect of O'Connor's relationship to Gaelic Ireland which must be considered is the one which is probably the most familiar to the general reader: his devotion to Irish poetry. In the course of a career lasting over forty years, he published verse translations of more than a hundred Irish poems of all periods; his first collection of such poems appeared in 1932 and the latest in 1963. He is almost certainly the single most important translator of Irish poetry into English in this century. As the poems in question range over a span of about twelve hundred years and represent at least three distinct stages of Irish, the degree of scholarship and concentration required to produce them was considerable. Modern readers with no Irish owe a large part of their knowledge of Irish poetry to O'Connor.

He was not, to be sure, equally enthusiastic about all periods of Irish poetry, any more than he was equally enamoured of all aspects of medieval architecture and decorative art. The professional court poetry of the later Middle Ages often seemed to him provincial and desiccated, and he disliked some of the eighteenth-century survivals of the bardic tradition. In keeping with his constant desire that Ireland should develop her own genius while at the same time looking out and ahead, he was particularly impressed with Irish art in periods when it was creating its own interpretations of impulses which had fairly recently come into the country from abroad. In one statement he tied together his response to poetry, his response to architectural ornamentation, and his views about modern Ireland.

A few weeks ago I spent some hours in the ruins of an Irish abbey. I saw there two tombs: one a Norman tomb of the thirteenth century after the defeat of the Irish. It shows two crusaders . . . I found it hard to contemplate without emotion the noble, sensuous flowing line, the delight in an ideal of human dignity and beauty. But beside that tomb stands another, from the fifteenth century when the Irish were again masters in their own house. It shows the twelve apostles; squat, lifeless, shapeless doll-like figures, their robes falling in stiff, geometrical folds, their faces without expression, with hard little beady eyes and hair and beards like wigs. It was a translation into stone of certain bardic poems of the time with all their cranky rules of thumb that rob the verse of any organic life. There was about them nothing that could delight the eye; not one glimmer of that sensuous beauty which had enchanted me in the Norman tomb. It was as though some Censor of the soul had wiped it out and replaced it by the angular, graceless lines of the

stone doll. . . . When the original tension created by conquest was
eased, there was no other tension to take its place, no straining after
a desirable vision of life, and the stretched sinew relaxed, content
with the (humanly-speaking) hideous mechanical grotesques of an
eighth-century illuminated manuscript.[38]

This passage, with its emphasis on 'human dignity and
beauty', certainly expresses O'Connor's own values, which
can perhaps best be summarized as liberal and humanist. The
stories which have been considered here are marked by an
openness to the *varieties* of human experience, impressive
whenever authentic. The prevailing conventions and the
social standing of the characters are not standards of value;
humanity itself is the touchstone. Thus O'Connor rejects any
art he regards as dehumanized. Nevertheless he gave the
literary and architectural work of all periods careful attention. His studies in these areas represent an attempt to come
to grips with a way of life almost totally unknown to Irish
people at the end of the nineteenth century. To dislike some
of it was not to imply that it should be ignored, certainly not
that it should be allowed to vanish. All of it had contributed
to the making of Ireland.

O'Connor's career viewed as a whole suggests that from
about the time of the Second World War, his own way of
resolving the problem of his relationship with Gaelic Ireland
was to concentrate on its *earlier* manifestations, literary or
architectural, rather than on the language issue or on such
other manifestations of the Gaelic tradition as remained
living in modern Ireland. His opposition to the official policy
of bilingualism did not prevent his occasionally writing and
broadcasting in Irish, even near the end of his life, but on the
whole in the later part of his career he appeared as a
transmitter and interpreter of older Gaelic culture for those
who had not yet apprehended it directly.

Near the end of his life he crystallized decades of work and
thought into a series of lectures given at Trinity College,
Dublin, on 'the literature of Ireland' from the earliest days up
to his own time. For O'Connor this meant a literature in Irish
up to the eighteenth century and a literature in English

thereafter; it was typical of him to want to bridge the gap between the two, accepting both as equally valid aspects of the Irish experience.

These lectures became the basis for a book published after his death under the title *The Backward Look*.[39] The title refers partly to the persistence in Irish literature of the theme of looking back at the past, a theme to which O'Connor himself did full justice in such elegaic stories as 'Uprooted', 'The Bridal Night', and 'The Majesty of the Law'. The title *The Backward Look* also of course refers to the author's own activity in looking back at the literature which led up to that of his own time. If his mature approach toward Gaelic Ireland was also largely that of the backward look, his justification for it may be found in the dedication of the book: 'For my children: look back to look forward'.

1. *An Only Child* (New York, 1961; London, 1962). Later page references are valid for either edition.
2. *My Father's Son* (London, 1968; New York, 1969). Later page references are to the London edition.
3. In *An Only Child*, O'Connor attacks de Valera for having left the interned men in a vacuum when he declared a cease fire but 'refused either to surrender or negotiate', p. 260. The internment experience was treated as early as 1934 in 'A Boy in Prison', *Life and Letters*, vol 10, no. 56, pp. 525–35, but this early article does not include the attack on de Valera.
4. *Guests of the Nation* (London and New York, 1931). Later page references are valid for either edition.
5. *Ibid.*, pp. 204–6. Compare the story with *An Only Child*, pp. 144–5.
6. 'Peasants', in *The Stories of Frank O'Connor* (New York, 1952; London, 1953), p. 154. This collection is hereafter referred to as *Stories*; page references are valid for either edition. 'Peasants' was first published in *Lovat Dickson's Magazine* (October, 1934) and was first collected in *Bones of Contention* (New York, 1936; London, 1938).
7. *Stories*, p. 155.
8. *Ibid.*, p. 161.
9. *My Father's Son*, pp. 54–5.
10. In *Bones of Contention* only.
11. *Stories*, p. 186. 'The Majesty of the Law' was first published in

Fortnightly Review (August, 1935) and collected in *Bones of Contention*.

12. *Stories*, pp. 181–2.
13. *Ibid.*, p. 180.
14. *Ibid.*, p. 178.
15. *Ibid.*, p. 164. 'In the Train' was first published in *Lovat Dickson's Magazine* (June, 1935) and was first collected in *Bones of Contention*.
16. *Stories*, p. 138. 'The Bridal Night' was first published in *Harper's Bazaar* (July, 1939) and was collected in *Crab Apple Jelly* (London and New York, 1944). Earlier it appeared in a limited edition, Frank O'Connor, *Three Tales* (Dublin, 1941).
17. *Stories*, p. 139.
18. *Ibid.*, p. 214. 'Uprooted' was first published in *Criterion* (January, 1937) and was first collected in *Crab Apple Jelly*.
19. *Stories*, p. 200.
20. *Ibid.*, p. 214.
21. *Ibid.*, pp. 214–15.
22. O'Connor published three short travel pieces about Ireland in a limited edition under the title *A Picture Book* (Dublin, 1943). They were later included in *Irish Miles* which is discussed below.
23. *Stories*, p. 197.
24. *Ibid.*, p. 129. 'The Long Road to Ummera' was first published in *The Bell* (October, 1940) and was first collected in *Crab Apple Jelly*. Compare the story with *An Only Child*, pp. 151–2, where O'Connor describes his grandmother's death.
25. *Stories*, p. 136.
26. 'The Old Faith' first appeared under the title 'The Soul of the Bishop' in *Argosy* (December, 1943). It was first collected in *More Stories by Frank O'Connor* (New York, 1954) and, in the British Isles in *Collection Two* (London, 1964).
27. *The Bookman*, vol. 86, 1934, p. 240.
28. *Ibid.*, p. 241.
29. *Ibid.*
30. Any significance for this choice of pseudonym is not immediately apparent. *Ben Mayo* sounds rather like the name of an Irish mountain. Mayo certainly gives associations with the life of the West of Ireland, and Ben might possibly suggest the outspoken quality of Benjamin Franklin's attempts to influence the young American nation.
31. See Hector Legge, 'When Frank O'Connor was Treated like an Outcast', *Sunday Independent*, 13 April 1969, p. 13.
32. 'Dublin is as "English" Today as it was Thirty Years Ago!', *Sunday Independent*, 28 January 1945, p. 3.

33. 'Timothy Buckley: A Memoir', *Irish Times*, 28 April 1945, p. 2.
34. Frank O'Connor, *Leinster, Munster and Connaught* (London, 1950), p. 195.
35. 28 March 1943, p. 1.
36. For example, see 'Our Crumbling Heritage – Restoration of our Monuments', colour supplement, 17 November 1963, pp. 4–6; 'Our Greatest Monument – Our Greatest Disgrace: Cashel', 21 June 1964, pp. 18–19; 'Shame on Us – Athassel Priory, Ennis Abbey, Dysert O'Dea, Quin Abbey', 12 July 1964, pp. 16–17.
37. *Irish Miles* (London, 1947).
38. 'The Stone Dolls', *The Bell*, vol. 2, no. 3, 1941, pp. 66–7.
39. *The Backward Look* (London, 1967); published in New York in the same year under the title *A Short History of Irish Literature: A Backward Look*.

Synge and 'The Aran Islands': a linguistic apprenticeship

MARY C. KING

From the time when Synge's plays first began to make their appearance on the stage in 1904, controversy has continued not merely about themes, plots and characters but also about the nature, appropriateness and 'authenticity' of the dramatic idiom. The riots associated with the 1907 production of *The Playboy of the Western World* are notorious. The play opened at the Abbey Theatre on Saturday, 26 January 1907, and was received with booing, cat-calls and violent interruptions. On the following Monday *The Freeman's Journal* published a scathing review of what it called 'the piece'. Of the dialogue, the reviewer wrote, 'The mere idea can be given of the barbarous jargon, the elaborate and incessant cursings of these repulsive creatures. Everything is a b————y this or a b————y that, and into the picturesque dialogue names that should only be used with respect and reverence are frequently introduced. Enough! the hideous caricature would be slanderous of a Kaffir kraal.'[1] A correspondent in the same edition of the *Journal*, who signed herself 'A Western Girl', declared that 'the play is stilted, impossible, uninteresting and un-Irish'. The *Evening Mail* reviewer, however, while critical of some of the 'coarse or blasphemous language' confessed to, 'drinking in every word of the dialogue with eager and excited interest and captivated by the rare charm and reality of the sayings and manners of his wonderful living Irish peasants'.[2]

Whatever may be the determining features of Synge's dramatic language, after he had completed his first, unperformed, play, *When the Moon has Set*, he never again drew substantially from a Standard English norm for his dramatic writings. The Irish English to which he turned was shaped, as Synge was aware, by many factors – by the social and cultural lives of the people who used it, by their daily work, by the time-span in history during which various groups of the native Irish people acquired English, and by the inevitable interference from the indigenous Gaelic tongue which, in Synge's time, had been virtually supplanted on the east coast (though relatively recently) by English. We know that Synge took a keen interest in language itself – not just in Gaelic, or English, or 'peasant speech', but also in the effects which an acquaintance with more than one language might have upon a person's view of life. His notebooks reveal an interest in the relationships between language, mythology, history, culture and society, and in the writer's function and craft as a user of words. Of the Aran Islanders themselves he noted

Foreign languages are another favourite topic, and as these men are bilingual they have a fair notion of what it means to speak and think in many different idioms. Most of the strangers they see on the islands are philological students, and the people have been led to conclude that linguistic studies and particularly Gaelic studies, are the chief occupation of the outside world.[3]

That Synge, therefore, did not spring strong-armed and bilingual from Yeats's brow is fairly well documented. In his book *Synge – a Critical Study of the Plays*[4] Nicholas Grene has summarized usefully the findings of Jiro Taniguchi and Nicholas Newlin on the main characteristics of the Irish–English dialect developed in the plays. I have myself examined elsewhere the interaction between Irish–Gaelic and Irish–English linguistic patterns and the development of theme and idiom in Synge's drama.[5] Much remains to be said, however, about the impact which direct, living experience of Irish–Gaelic/Irish–English bilingualism had upon Synge himself, when he began, during his visits to Aran, to develop his practical skills as a Gaelic speaker and to observe at first-hand the impact of a 'reverse' bilingualism on the Islanders, as their contact with speakers of English began to expand. As this chapter will seek to show, the experience placed Synge in a uniquely favourable situation in which his attention was sharply focused, because of his previous acquaintance with Celtic languages and Celtic studies, on the *nature* of language and its relationship both to everyday realities and to an ancient, still surviving, but changing culture with which he sought identification and from which he was equally, and ironically, aware of his separateness and the value of that separation. As Nicholas Grene rightly points out, in Synge's plays 'the attitude to language is itself a major theme'.[6] The seeds of this attitude were sown academically during Synge's studies at Trinity and later, at the Sorbonne. They germinated during his Aran Island apprenticeship and as he himself suggested, they flowered and bore fruit, in theme and style, in the plays, in ways which have yet to be adequately recognized.

Synge's preoccupation specifically with Irish Gaelic showed itself early in his career. It is indicated by his choice of Gaelic as a subject of study at Trinity College Dublin and by his winning a medal for his achievements. It is characteristic of him that his studies of Gaelic were not restricted to the language alone, but embraced a desire to find out from primary sources about Celtic history, traditions and literature. It is probably true to say that such a concern was part of the search for an identity which affected many artists at the end of the nineteenth century. For historical reasons this took a particularly urgent form for the Young Protestant Anglo-Irish intellectuals from the declining ascendancy families. Synge certainly appears to have been dissatisfied with what was offered in Celtic studies at Trinity, complaining that if

an odd undergraduate . . . wished to learn a little of the Irish language . . . he found an amiable old clergyman who made him read a crabbed version of the New Testament, and seemed to know nothing, or at least to care nothing, about the old literature of Ireland, or the fine folk tales and folk poetry of Munster and Connaught.[7]

Synge comments in his fragmentary autobiography on his early acquisition of a scientific attitude of mind, through his reading of Darwin and his study of insects. He was not one to be easily satisfied by the vague, romantic, Ossianic celticism of his fellow Wicklow writer, Thomas Moore, and, to a

certain extent, of the younger Yeats. He is reported to have
said, half jocularly once, of Yeats that 'Yeats looks after the
stars and I look after the rest'. When he abandoned his music
studies in Germany and went to Paris, he resumed formally
his study of Celtic languages and culture at the Sorbonne in
1895. The records in his notebooks over the period 1891–
1902 are not full enough to enable one to assess the level of
his mastery of Irish Gaelic, although it is possible to notice
his developing skill in using the modified Gothic script, and a
degree of progress is obvious in the complexity of the
composition exercises attempted. We know from his Trinity
diary of 1892 that he had read the Irish Gaelic texts of 'Lir'
and 'Diarmuid and Grainne' in that year, though very
slowly. It is unlikely that he acquired much facility in the
spoken language of Irish Gaelic before his first visit to Aran
in 1898, but he was by then well equipped with an understanding of the structure, syntax and diachronic development
of Irish Gaelic, and had acquired an acquaintance with
Breton. It is reasonable to assume that this knowledge would
have alerted him to significant structural features of Gaelic
and to the possible effects of these upon the Aran Islanders'
and Wicklow peasants' use of English.

Before Synge's first visit to Aran, however, there is little
evidence, either in the notebooks or the other writings, of
any direct linguistic influence upon his style from his studies
of Celtic languages. The concern reflected in the notebooks is
more with the philosophical implications of Celtic mythology and its relationship to the European tradition and it was
not until sixteen months after his meeting with Yeats in Paris
in December 1896 that he finally went to the Aran Islands.
Before doing so he attended yet another course of lectures
given in Paris by Professor H. d'Arbois de Jubainville 'sur la
civilisation irlandaise comparée avec celle d'Homer'. He
arrived on Aran Mór on 10 May 1898, and was to remain on
the Islands, on this occasion, for six weeks.

Greene and Stephens remark that Synge brought with him
to the Aran Islands 'a linguistic equipment which his col-
leagues could only envy and an insight sharpened by his

knowledge of Continental Celticism'.[8] It is, however, noticeable that when he first arrived on Aran Mór, Synge had
difficulty understanding spoken Irish Gaelic. Many of the
references to language in the first part of 'The Aran Islands'
mention the 'murmur of Gaelic';[9] the 'sort of chant'; the
'exquisite purity of intonation that brought tears to my eyes,
though I understand but little of their meaning' (p. 56); the
'continual drone of Gaelic' (p. 57); 'a faint murmur of Gaelic'
(p. 82); 'a fierce rhapsody in Gaelic' (p. 92). He comments
explicitly on the problems which he had understanding Irish
Gaelic, and when Pat Dirane told him the story upon which
The Shadow of the Glen is partly based, he narrated it in
English. Synge also writes that he himself was unable to
follow the 'moral dispute' which ensued, as 'unfortunately it
was carried on so rapidly in Gaelic that I lost most of the
points' (p. 61). On Aran Mór he was 'in general . . . surprised
at the abundance and fluency of the foreign tongue' (p. 50) (i.e.
English) and his attention at the beginning seems to have been
directed linguistically more to the characteristics of the Islanders' English than to the syntax or semantics of Gaelic, which
appears to hold his interest more for its tone patterns and
cadences. Indeed, he ruefully remarks, when he listens to the
gulls crying, that 'their language is easier than Gaelic' (p. 73).

Of the Islanders' English Synge notes that it is a 'curiously
simple yet dignified language', 'careful English' (p. 53); that
'a few of the men have a curiously full vocabulary, others
know only the commonest words in English and are driven
to ingenious devices to express their meaning' (p. 60). Soon,
however, he begins to make tentative comparisons between
Irish Gaelic and the English which he hears: 'Some of them
express themselves more correctly than the ordinary peasant,
others use the Gaelic idioms continually and substitute "he"
or "she" for "it" as the neuter pronoun is not found in
modern Irish' (p. 60). More important, perhaps, for our
interest in the evolution of his dramatic language, we find
Synge, as part one of 'The Aran Islands' progresses, integrating into the narrative text examples of the linguistic characteristics which he notices, so that the language patterns,

syntactic, lexical and phonological, which will be built upon in his plays, begin to emerge, together with some of the thematic material. As an example of the 'curiously simple yet dignified language' he gives the complaint of the old man who told him 'I have come back to live in a bit of a house with my sister. The island is not the same at all to what it was. It is little good I can get from the people who are in it now, and anything I have to give them they don't care to have' (p. 53). He illustrates the 'ingenious' syntactic devices with the words of the man impressed by the visits of antiquarians and philologists to the Islands: 'I have seen Frenchmen, and Danes, and Germans, and there does be a power of Irish books along with them, and they reading them better than ourselves. Believe me, there are few rich men now in the world who are not studying the Gaelic' (p. 60). What is interesting here is that there are no features, either grammatical or lexical, in the above extracts which I find in any way different from the language used by older country people in County Wicklow today. The utterances would not seem at all unusual linguistically to me if spoken, for example, by my own father. It would appear, therefore, that what is happening to Synge is the development of a new *awareness* of Irish English.

The gathering and presentation of the 'set pieces' in part one of 'The Aran Islands', the folktales, gave Synge his most sustained linguistic practice to date at recording, imitating and developing his own version of spoken forms. Undoubtedly also, this experience contributed to his sense of the dramatic, in terms of both content and technique. J. H. Delargy in his study 'The Gaelic Storyteller' makes several points which are valuable for an appreciation of the technical skills which a dramatist might stand to gain from an acquaintance with traditional storytelling:

The tale that is not told dies; the storyteller without an audience remains passive, and his tales die with him. For the art of the folktale is in its telling; it was never meant to be written nor to be read. It draws the breath of life from the lips of men and from the applause of the appreciative fireside audience.[10]

Delargy emphasizes the shared sense of the structured aesthetic of traditional dialogue techniques, between teller and audience:

A characteristic feature of early and medieval Irish prose narrative is the effective and skilful use of dialogue, and this is very marked in the modern Gaelic folktale . . . A good storyteller rarely departs from *oratio recta* in the first telling of a tale . . . The best type of storyteller rarely departs from traditional usage in this respect, as he appreciates how much well-constructed dialogue can add to the effect of his tale on a critical audience, familiar themselves by everyday practice with witty, epigrammatic talk and telling riposte. As W. P. Ker remarks, the old saga-style was essentially conversational; the same may be said of the modern Irish folktale.[11]

If Synge's diaries record only two visits to the 'institutional' theatre before 1905, during his Aran visits opportunities to serve a dramatic apprenticeship were not lacking.

As part one of 'The Aran Islands' progresses, we find Synge becoming more self-assured in Gaelic, recording how he was able, himself, to join in the 'ripostes':

'Is it tired you are, stranger?' said one girl.

'Bedad, it is not, little girl,' I answered *in Gaelic*, 'it is lonely I am.'[12]

By the time the first part draws to a close, he is confident enough in his movement from one language to the other to render more frequently in direct speech the words which the Islanders spoke in their own tongue:

An old woman came . . . forward from the crowd and, mounting on a rock near the ship, began a fierce rhapsody *in Gaelic*, pointing at the bailiff and waving her withered arms with extraordinary rage. 'This is my own son,' she said, it is I that ought to know him. He is the first ruffian *in the whole big world.*[13]

There last words anticipate *The Playboy of the Western World*. As if to emphasize both his debt to the Islanders' bilingualism and his newly acquired skill, Synge concludes part one with a letter to him from a young boy 'beginning in Irish and ending . . . in English'.[14]

Parts two, three and four of 'The Aran Islands' record Synge's return visits in the years 1899, 1900 and 1901 respectively. Linguistically, there is a noticeable and carefully structured progression throughout each part and from one part to the next. It is worth remembering in this context that Synge wrote of this work that

> I look on 'The Aran Islands' as my first serious piece of work – it was written before any of my plays. In writing out the talk of the people and their stories in this book, and in a certain number of articles on the Wicklow peasantry . . . I learned to write the peasant dialect which I use in my plays . . . 'The Aran Islands' throws a good deal of light on my plays.[15]

Parts two and three record no 'set' folktales whatever: Synge would appear to be indicating his greater ease in the direct recording of daily events, the drama and conversation, both Gaelic and English, of Island life. In part two he has become noticeably more of a participant. He records, from a girl with whom he had many conversations, language and sentiments which Nora is to echo in *The Shadow of the Glen*:

> 'Ah, it's a queer place,' she said; 'I wouldn't choose to live in it. It's a queer place, and indeed I don't know the place that isn't . . .'
> 'Father X is gone,' she said; 'he was a kind man but a queer man. Priests is queer people, and I don't know who isn't (p. 114).

So confident and linguistically integrated has Synge become that he now joins freely in the exchanges, and the Islanders can tease and jest with him. There are no further comments about difficulties with Gaelic; rather, Synge appears to have mastered the rendering of Irish Gaelic into English:

> 'Whisper, noble person,' he began, 'do you never be thinking on the young girls? The time I was a young man the devil a one of them could I look on without wishing to marry her.' 'Ah Mourteen,' I answered, 'it's a great wonder you'd be asking me. What at all do you think of me yourself? (p. 121).

Or again:

> 'It's real heavy she is, your honour,' he said. 'I'm thinking it's gold there will be in it.'
> 'Divil a ha'porth is there in it at all but books,' I answered him in Gaelic (p. 121).

Part three opens with Synge calling attention directly to the nature of the language he is using – through Micheál's two letters to him in Paris, one in a more 'rhetorical mood' than the other. He describes also in this section the aesthetic sense of language in the young boy who came up each afternoon to read to him in Gaelic from a dual language edition of Douglas Hyde's folktale collection, *Beside the Fire*:

'There's a mistake in the English,' he said after a moment's hesitation; 'he's put "gold chair" instead of "golden chair".' I pointed out that we would speak of gold watches and gold pins. 'And why wouldn't we?' he said, 'but "golden chairs" would be much nicer.'

It is curious to see how his rudimentary culture had given him the beginning of a critical spirit that occupies itself with the form of the language as well as with ideas (p. 133).

Synge also tells of the old man who 'was ready to rise up and criticise an eminent dignitary and scholar on rather delicate points of versification, and the finer distinctions between old words of Gaelic' (p. 149). He records the important observation that 'the people have so few images for description that they seize on anything that is remarkable in their visitors and use it afterwards in their talk' (p. 129) an observation full of interest to any student of Synge's dramatic use of imagery. The text now stresses more than before a conscious response to features of the Islanders' speech:

I was surprised to notice that several women who professed to know no English could make themselves understood without difficulty when it pleased them. 'The rings is too dear at you, sir,' said one girl, *using the Gaelic construction*; 'let you put less money on them and all the girls will be buying them.'[16]

I stood and talked with them in Irish, as I was anxious *to compare their language* and temperament with that I knew of the other island.[17]

She plays continual tricks with her Gaelic in the way girls are fond of, *piling up diminutives and repeating adjectives with a humorous scorn of syntax*.[18]

Part three concludes, however, with an anecdote which bears witness to a totally unsentimental attitude to language, suggesting an awareness, which Synge expresses explicitly elsewhere, that Irish Gaelic is destined not to survive as a living language.

Part four returns to the patterns of storytelling found in the first section. Synge is now even more at home, if temporarily, with the people, providing music for the Islanders to dance to, which is remarkable when we recall his painful shyness about playing the violin in public. His own great 'set piece', which holds the centre of this movement is the dramatic description of the Island funeral, which later was to provide him with material for *Riders to the Sea*. It is set in a series of stories told him by the Islanders of dead men and great riders. The concluding section emphasizes his craftsman's interest both in Gaelic and in the Islanders' use of English, this time in literary discourse. We are reminded of the literary apprenticeship he is serving when he records a long 'extraordinary English doggerel rhyme . . . These rhymes are repeated by the old men as a sort of chant', and he follows this almost immediately with two translations of poems, 'Rucard Mór', 'as near the Irish as I am able to make it' (p. 172) and 'Phelim and the Eagle', a corporate effort undertaken by himself and a scholar visitor to the Islands. Now, also, Synge records his confidence and expertise in joining in the traditional telling of folktales, and exchanging stories with the man who informs him of the magical properties of the *De Profundis* – a power invoked by the Tramp in *The Shadow of the Glen*. 'I told him', writes Synge, 'the story of the fairy ship which had disappeared when the man made the sign of the cross, *as I heard it on the middle island.*'[19]

Towards the end of 'The Aran Islands' we find an interesting, and rare, use of the integrating 'we', as if Synge wishes to confirm his sense of identity with the people on his last night on the Islands: 'This evening we had a dance in the inn parlour' (p. 182). But Synge was never a man for facile presumption or romantic self-delusion. His sense of irony is rarely far away. He brings his account of his apprenticeship to an end by progressively distancing himself from the

Islanders, providing us, finally, with a translation of a folk-riddle which reflects back sardonically on himself and his new-found knowledge – a riddle which we might well recall in the context of the drink imagery in the plays:

This is what the old woman says at Beulleaca when she sees a man without knowledge – Were you ever at the house of the still, did you ever get a drink from it? Neither wine nor beer is as sweet as it is, but it is well I was not burnt when I fell down after a drink of it by the fire of Mr. Sloper. 'I praise Owen O'Hernon over all the doctors of Ireland, it is he put drugs on the water, and it lying on the barley.

'If you gave but a drop of it to an old woman who does be walking the world with a stick, she would think for a week that it was a fine bed was made for her (p. 184).

Having drunk their fill of whiskey, the Islanders return to their homes, fearful of the fairies. Synge, meanwhile, withdraws from the Still of Aran and its linguistic intoxication, having drunk enough to praise the 'drugs on the water', but before he himself is burnt by the fire like Christy in *The Playboy of the Western World*. He briefly and wryly concludes, 'The next day I left with the steamer' (p. 184).

My thanks are due to the staff of the Manuscript Room, Trinity College, Dublin, for facilitating my readings of the Synge Papers in their collection over the past two years.

1. Quoted in James Kilroy, *The Playboy Riots* (Dublin, 1971), p. 9.
2. *Ibid.*, p. 13.
3. J. M. Synge, 'The Aran Islands' in *Collected Works*, vol. 2, *Prose*, ed. Alan Price (London, 1966), p. 60. In connection with Synge's comment here on bilingualism, it is interesting to note that his own diary for the period May–June 1898 recording his first visit to Aran is written almost exclusively in French.
4. Nicholas Grene, *Synge: A Critical Study of the Plays* (London, 1975).
5. In 'Towards a Dramatic Idiom: 'Language and Style in J. M. Synge's *The Shadow of the Glen*' – unpublished MA dissertation, University of Leeds (1976).
6. Grene, *Synge: A Critical Study*, p. 83.
7. Synge, 'Aran Islands', p. 384.

8. David H. Greene and E. M. Stephens, *J. M. Synge: Biography* (New York, 1959), p. 65.
9. Synge, 'Aran Islands', p. 49.
10. J. H. Delargy, 'The Gaelic Storyteller', in *Proceedings of the British Academy* (1945), p. 187.
11. *Ibid.*, p. 207.
12. Synge, 'Aran Islands', p. 83 (my italics).
13. *Ibid.*, p. 92 (my italics).
14. *Ibid.*, p. 103.
15. Synge, in unpublished letters to Spencer Brodney, quoted in footnote to 'Aran Islands', p. 47.
16. *Ibid.*, p. 138 (my italics).
17. *Ibid.*, p. 140 (my italics).
18. *Ibid.*, p. 143 (my italics).
19. *Ibid.*, p. 181 (my italics).

Yeats's fishermen and Samuel Ferguson's 'Willy Gilliland'

DAVID R. CLARK

When Yeats composed 'The Fisherman'[1] he was still under the influence of the nationalist rhetoric which clothed his hero in 'grey Connemara cloth'.[2] By 1922 he could comment in disillusion on his own wearing of homespun in the nineties: 'I believed myself dressed according to public opinion, until a letter of apology from my tailor informed me that "It takes such a long time getting Connemara cloth as it has to come all the way from Scotland." '[3] Ironically, Yeats's fishermen may have come from Scotland too. As we shall see, Samuel Ferguson's 'Willy Gilliland' may have suggested the fisherman figure.

The fishermen of 'The Tower'[4] are not western country-men in a uniform of grey Connemara cloth, but Anglo-Irish Protestants, and, as has often been pointed out, Yeats's description of them as 'The people of Burke and of Grattan' echoes his 11 June 1925 defence of the Protestant minority in the Senate debate on divorce: 'We against whom you have done this thing are no petty people. We are one of the great stocks of Europe. We are the people of Burke; we are the people of Grattan; we are the people of Swift, the people of Emmet, the people of Parnell.'[5] To Ireland, all these Anglo-Irishmen 'gave, though free to refuse'.[6]

Yeats was discovering and declaring for his Anglo-Irish heritage. 'We have created the most of the modern literature of this country. We have created the best of its political intelligence . . . You have defined our position and given us a popular following. If we have not lost our stamina then your victory will be brief, and your defeat final, and when it comes this nation may be transformed.'[7]

What transformation did Yeats hope for? He had summarized the history of Irish political attitudes in 'The Stirring of the Bones'. 'A movement first of poetry, then of sentimentality, and land hunger, had struggled with, and as the nation passed into the second period of all revolutions given way before a movement of abstraction and hatred; and after some twenty years of the second period, though abstraction and hatred have won their victory, there is no clear sign, of a third, a *tertium quid*, and a reasonable frame of mind.'[8] Such a transformation might come, however, if minorities would resist the attempts of fanaticism upon their liberties. 'I want those minorities to resist', Yeats wrote in March 1925, 'and their resistance may do an overwhelming service to this country, they may become the centre of its creative intellect and the pivot of its unity . . . We must become a modern, tolerant, liberal nation.'[9]

'Only the individual soul can attain to its spiritual opposite.' Therefore 'a nation in tumult must needs pass to and fro between mechanical opposites'.[10] It is the stance of the individual soul with which Yeats is concerned in his fishermen, and Protestantism is as irrelevant as grey Connemara cloth to what he is really saying.

The model for the rhetorical structure of 'The Fisherman', T. McAlindon has pointed out, was Shakespeare's sonnet 66, 'Tired with all these, for restful death I cry', quoted in full in Yeats's 1901 essay 'At Stratford-on-Avon'. For Yeats, says McAlindon, 'Shakespeare was a poet of the old order who valued men for what they are in themselves and not for their practical utility.' Yeats's Shakespeare saw 'a disastrous change that was to be accomplished in his own time, the change from a courtly to a democratic ethos' and 'The Fisherman' is Yeats's 'own pessimistic vision of democratic reality'. As opposed to Bolingbroke, Richard II is 'represented as the personification of disinterested art . . . and is even identified with the Fountain of Life: "that lyricism which rose out of Richard's mind like the jet of a fountain to fall again where it had risen . . . that fantasy too enfolded in its own sincerity to make any thought the hour had need of . . ."' This image McAlindon finds again in the 'abounding glittering jet' of 'Ancestral Houses'.[11]

Skilful in fly-casting, Yeats's heirs in 'The Tower' who 'climb the streams until / The fountain leap, and at dawn / Drop their cast at the side / Of dripping stone'[12] and 'The Fisherman' who climbs 'up to a place / Where stone is dark under froth'[13] are also personifications of disinterested art and are sources of national culture. 'England . . . was made by her adventurers, by her people of wildness and imagination and eccentricity',[14] and such persons are the hope of Ireland too though 'the wise' and 'great Art' are 'beaten down' by the mob: 'The Accusation of Sin produced its necessary fruit, hatred of all that was abundant, extravagant, exuberant, of all that sets a sail for shipwreck, and flattery of the common-place emotions and conventional ideals of the mob, the chief Paymaster of accusation'.[15]

Richard II, the fisherman in grey Connemara cloth, the idealized Protestants of the Senate speech, the 'young up-standing' Anglo-Irishmen of 'The Tower' are all 'full' (and overflowing) men standing against the 'empty' men of the mob – whether Bolingbrokes, Paudeens fumbling 'in a greasy till',[16] or fanatic religionists. Such a 'full' man was Ferguson's Willy Gilliland, standing against his 'empty' Episcopalian persecutors.

It has been pointed out that Yeats's middle and late poems sometimes echo poems and ballads by Thomas Davis and the Young Ireland poets, by James Clarence Mangan and Sir Samuel Ferguson, which preoccupy some of Yeats's early criticism but are less often referred to later on.[17] No one, I think, has shown the relationship of Yeats's 'The Fisherman' and of the first and third parts of 'The Tower' to Ferguson's 'Willy Gilliland'[18] – that the fisherman's 'grey Connemara cloth' may originally have been a Scots kirkman's blue bonnet. In his first essay on Ferguson Yeats excuses himself from quoting 'that ringing ballad, "Willy Gilliland"'. 'I could give no idea of a fine building by showing a carved flower from a cornice.'[19] He classifies it as one of those poems 'in which character is subordinated to some dominant idea or event'.[20]

The dominant event is the interruption of a fishing idyll by English troops bent on religious persecution. Willy Gilliland is a Covenanter who 'has worshipp'd God upon the hill, in spite of church and king'.[21] He has fought King Charles's forces at the battle of Bothwell Bridge (1679) and in retaliation the family farm has been one of those burned by soldiers commanded by John Graham of Claverhouse (1649?–89) and Thomas Dalyell or Dalzell (1599?–1685). He has fled Scotland and taken shelter in northeastern Ireland and it is not Connemara but Antrim which is the setting for Ferguson's poem. Persecution follows Willy to Carrickfergus.

> His name was on the Carrick cross, a price was on
>   his head,
> A fortune to the man that brings him in alive or
>   dead!
> And so on moor and mountain, from the Lagan to
>   the Bann,
> From house to house, and hill to hill, he lurk'd an
>   outlaw'd man.

At last he leaves 'false company' and lives alone in a cave 'upon the Collon side', in Glenwhirry, subsisting on the country.

> With hound and fishing-rod he lived on hill and
>   stream by day;
> At night, betwixt his fleet greyhound and his bonny
>   mare he lay.[22]

Glenwhirry is 'a parish in Antrim, taking its name from the river which runs by Kells into the Main'.[23] Thus it would be situated perhaps five miles north of Antrim and less than twenty miles northwest of Carrickfergus. It is an area for which Ferguson felt nostalgia. He writes, 'During my childhood the family resided at . . . Collon in Glenwhirry, where I received those impressions of Nature and romance which have more or less influenced all my habits of thought and sentiment in after-life.'[24] Glenwhirry cannot be far from the original seat of the Ferguson family and the spot where Ferguson chose to be buried. The landscape in the following description is much like Glenwhirry as described in the poem:

The Ferguson property was situated in and about the valley of the Six-Mile Water, which empties itself into Lough Neagh near the town of Antrim. Here stands one of the earliest of the Irish round towers, and not far distant may be traced the remains of the royal fort of Rathmore–Moy-Linny. The region is dominated by the moat of Donegore. This fine earthwork is a conspicuous object in the landscape. It commands an extensive view over a rich and undulating country to Lough Neagh, with its expanse of waters and boundary of distant mountains. To the north rise the Connor Hills and the wedge-like mountain of Slemish. At the base of the moat, or rath, stands the pretty church of Donegore. Here, on its lower slopes included in the churchyard, is the burying-place of the Ferguson family, and in this plot of ground repose the mortal remains of the Poet . . .[25]

> It was a summer evening, and, mellowing and still,
> Glenwhirry to the setting sun lay bare from hill to hill;
> For all that valley pastoral held neither house nor tree,
> But spread abroad and open all, a full fair sight to see,
> From Slemish foot to Collon top lay one unbroken green,
> Save where in many a silver coil the river glanced between.[26]

Like Yeats, Ferguson remembers that he was 'of that metal made / Till it was broken by / This sedentary trade',[27] and the opening section of 'The Tower' recalls the Ferguson poem:

> Never had I more
> Excited, passionate, fantastical
> Imagination, nor an ear and eye
> That more expected the impossible –
> No, not in boyhood when with rod and fly,
> Or the humbler worm, I climbed Ben Bulben's back
> And had the livelong summer day to spend.[28]

> And on the river's grassy bank, even from the
>   morning grey,
> He at the angler's pleasant sport had spent the
>   summer day:
> Ah! many a time and oft I've spent the summer
>   day from dawn,
> And wonder'd, when the sunset came, where time
>   and care had gone,

> Along the reaches curling fresh, the wimpling pools
>   and streams,
> Where he that day his cares forgot in those delightful
>   dreams.[29]

Coming back to his cave on Collon, Willy spies troopers
there. They go off 'with three long yells at parting', having
burnt his bed, killed his hound, and stolen his broadsword
and his 'bonny mare'. The worst stanza of the poem shows
the angry Scot vowing vengeance:

> 'My bonny mare! I've ridden you when Claver'se
>   rode behind,
> And from the thumbscrew and the boot you bore me
>   like the wind;
> And, while I have the life you saved, on your sleek
>   flank, I swear,
> Episcopalian rowel shall never ruffle hair!
> Though sword to wield they've left me none – yet
>   Wallace wight, I wis,
> Good battle did on Irvine side wi' waur weapon
>   than this' – [30]

His fishing rod of iron has a tough hickory butt. He breaks
off the long slender top and grinds the iron spike that remains
to a sharp point. Thus armed, he strides off to Carrickfergus,
lies in wait through two dawns for the troopers to emerge,
kills the man who rides on his mare, and escapes pursuit,
drawing rein at last on 'Skerry side' in Glenwhirry.

Willy lives, on this very spot, to become a landowner; yet
in other respects he is like Yeats's fisherman, a proud
freedom-loving man.

> Ah! little thought Willy Gilliland, when he on
>   Skerry side
> Drew bridle first, and wiped his brow after that
>   weary ride,
> That where he lay like hunted brute, a cavern'd
>   outlaw lone,
> Broad lands and yeoman tenantry should yet be
>   there his own:
> Yet so it was; and still from him descendants not
>   a few
> Draw birth and lands, and, let me trust, draw love
>   of Freedom too.[31]

Like Yeats's fishermen, Willy Gilliland is a solitary. 'In false company he might no longer bide.' He is one against many, and those many are common and comic urban figures:

> And now the gates are open'd, and forth in gallant
>   show
> Prick jeering grooms and burghers blythe, and
>   troopers in a row;
> But one has little care for jest, so hard bested
>   is he,
> To ride the outlaw's bonny mare, for this at last is
>   she![32]

Willy and Yeats's fishermen are lonely, heroic, potentially tragic figures, poised against a pack of clowns.

> The insolent unreproved,
> And no knave brought to book
> Who has won a drunken cheer,
> The witty man and his joke
> Aimed at the commonest ear,
> The clever man who cries
> The catch-cries of the clown. . .[33]

The symbolic landscape is similar in the three poems. Yeats's solitaries go 'to a grey place on a hill',[34] 'climb the streams',[35] or 'the mountain-side',[36] just as Willy begins 'Up in the mountain solitudes'. They climb up to a source symbolic of their true traditionalism and originality, 'Climbing up to a place / Where stone is dark under froth'[37] 'until / The fountain leap'.[38] So Ferguson has fished 'Along the reaches curling fresh, the wimpling pools and streams, / Where he [Willy] that day his cares forgot in those delightful dreams'.[39] It is on 'the river's grassy bank' that Willy fills 'the lonely valley with the gladsome word of God'.[40] At the last Willy is himself a source from whom descendants draw 'birth and lands' and 'love of Freedom'.[41]

We may expect fishermen to start out at dawn, but in these poems the hour symbolizes a pure day-spring quality, an originality they all have. It is 'a wise and simple man' who goes 'At dawn to cast his flies'.[42] They are 'upstanding men' who 'at dawn / Drop their cast at the side / Of dripping stone'. They have 'Pride, like that of the morn, / When the headlong light is loose'.[43] It is 'under bursting dawn' that 'They may drop a fly'.[44] Willy has been 'on the river's grassy bank, even from the morning grey'.[45] Later Willy is at his station when

> The sun shines bright on Carrick wall and Carrick
>   Castle grey,
> And up thine aisle, St. Nicholas, has ta'en his
>   morning way,
> And to the North-Gate sentinel displayeth far and
>   near
> Sea, hill, and tower, and all thereon, in dewy
>   freshness clear . . .[46]

He has to wait through this day and another dawn for the gates to open and the troopers to ride out so that he can commit his heroic deed.

In all three poems we see the 'young upstanding men' through the eyes of an older sedentary writer who idealizes them. And in all three poems – 'The Fisherman,' 'The Tower,' and 'Willy Gilliland' – the ideal is of a proud, self-reliant, freedom-loving individual. Willy is like the Yeatsian hero in acting, in this instance, on a personal rather than a public principle, following a subjective 'whim' rather than an objective 'task'.[47] Bound to the cause of the Covenant, he flees and flees from persecution. But when his persecutors kill his dog and steal his sword and mare, he cries, 'The Philistines!' – have they violated his religious code or his code of manners and aesthetics? – and fights them with implacable courage and with 'Pride, like that of the morn, / When the headlong light is loose'.

'Radical innocence' is what all Yeats's heroes have. Their souls are 'self-delighting, / Self-appeasing, self-affrighting'.[48] They are 'Bound neither to Cause nor to State'.[49] 'Nor law, nor duty bade' them fight[50] any more than they did Willy Gilliland, who finally fought not so much for Scotch Presbyterianism as for his mount, that is for his own pride. Greatness of soul is what Yeats saw in his heroes as he saw it in Willy Gilliland's author, Samuel Ferguson, whose

work he described – as he described the minds of Richard II
and the fishermen – in terms of the leaping fountain:

Sir Samuel Ferguson's special claim to our attention is that he went
back to the Irish cycle, finding it, in truth, a fountain that, in the
passage of centuries, was overgrown with weeds and grass, so that
the very way to it was forgotten of the poets; but now that his feet
have worn the pathway, many others will follow, and bring thence
living waters for the healing of our nation, helping us to live the
larger life of the Spirit, and lifting our souls away from their selfish
joys and sorrows to be the companions of those who lived greatly
among the woods and hills when the world was young.[51]

1. Dated 4 June 1914, by Richard Ellmann, *The Identity of Yeats*
   (New York, 1954), p. 290.
2. 'The Fisherman', *The Variorum Edition of the Poems of W. B.
   Yeats*, ed. Peter Allt and Russell K. Alspach (New York, 1957),
   p. 348. Yeats was also under the influence of Synge's presentation of the Aran islander and of Jack Yeats's illustration 'An
   Island Man'. J. M. Synge, *Collected Works*, vol. 2, *Prose*, ed.
   Alan Price (London, 1966), pp. 46, 59, 66, 132–33. The phrase
   'great Art beaten down' is reminiscent of Wordsworth's 'And
   mighty Poets in their misery dead', but I do not believe that
   Yeats was 'rewriting' Wordsworth as claims Shyamal Bag-
   chee, in his 'Anxiety of Influence: "Resolution and Independence" and Yeats's "The Fisherman",' *Yeats Eliot Review*, vol.
   5, no. 1, 1978, 51–7.
3. *The Autobiography of William Butler Yeats* (New York, 1971),
   p. 240. A. N. Jeffares, *A Commentary on the Collected Poems of
   W. B. Yeats* (London, 1968), p. 180, points out this comment.
4. Dated 7 October 1925, by Ellmann, *The Identity of Yeats*, p.
   291.
5. *The Senate Speeches of W. B. Yeats*, ed. Donald R. Pearce
   (Bloomington, 1960), p. 99.
6. *The Variorum Edition of the Poems of W. B. Yeats*, p. 414.
7. *The Senate Speeches of W. B. Yeats*, p. 99.
8. *The Autobiography of William Butler Yeats*, p. 239.
9. *The Senate Speeches of W. B. Yeats*, pp. 159–60.
10. *The Autobiography of William Butler Yeats*, p. 239.
11. T. McAlindon, 'Yeats and the English Renaissance', *PMLA*,
    vol. 82, no. 2, 1967, 157–69; especially pp. 159–60. W. B.
    Yeats, *Essays and Introductions* (New York, 1961), p. 108.
12. *The Variorum Edition of the Poems of W. B. Yeats*, p. 414.
13. *Ibid.*, p. 348.

14. W. B. Yeats, *Essays and Introductions*, p. 104.
15. *Ibid.*, p. 105.
16. *The Variorum Edition of the Poems of W. B. Yeats*, p. 289.
17. The most striking example is the use of Ferguson's *Congal* (1872), discussed by Yeats in his first published article, 'Irish Poets and Irish Poetry', *The Irish Fireside*, 9 October 1886. Cf. *Uncollected Prose by W. B. Yeats*, vol. 1, ed. John P. Frayne (London, 1970), pp. 81–7. *Congal* is the basis of the plot of *The Herne's Egg* (1938). Cf. *The Herne's Egg and Other Plays* (New York, 1938), p. v. Other echoes, also survivals of his early twenties, are pointed out in George S. Fraser, 'Yeats and the Ballad Style', *Shenandoah* (Washington and Lee University Review) vol. 21, no. 3, 1970, 186; David R. Clark, *Lyric Resonance* (Amherst, 1972), pp. 19–21; Colin Meir, *The Ballads and Songs of W. B. Yeats* (London, 1974), pp. 118–21; Robert O'Driscoll, *An Ascendancy of the Heart* (Toronto, 1976), pp. 60–1.
18. Samuel Ferguson, 'Willy Gilliland: An Ulster Ballad', *Lays of the Western Gael, and Other Poems* (London, 1865), pp. 110–18.
19. *Uncollected Prose by W. B. Yeats*, 1, pp. 83–4.
20. *Ibid.*, 1, 82.
21. Ferguson, 'Willy Gilliland: An Ulster Ballad', p. 110.
22. *Ibid.*, p. 111.
23. P. W. Joyce, *The Origin and History of Irish Names of Places*, seventh edition, in two volumes (Dublin and London, 1898), vol. 1, p. 53. Joyce continues, 'It is called Glancurry in the Inquisitions, and its Irish name is *Gleann-a'-choire*, the glen of the river Curry, or *Coire*, this last name signifying a caldron. The caldron is a deep pool formed under a cataract; and a rocky hill near it is called *Sceir-a'-choire*, the rock of the caldron, which, in the modernized form Skerrywhirry, is the name of a townland'. It is to 'Skerry side' – obviously near Glenwhirry – that Willy escapes at the end of the poem. Ferguson, 'Willy Gilliland: An Ulster Ballad', p. 118.
24. Lady Ferguson, *Sir Samuel Ferguson in the Ireland of His Day*, in two volumes (Edinburgh and London, 1896), 1, p. 4.
25. *Ibid.*, 1, p. 2.
26. Samuel Ferguson, 'Willy Gilliland: An Ulster Ballad', pp. 111–12. An 'Historical Notice of the Parish and People of Donegore', quoted by Lady Ferguson, tells that the Fergusons, like the Gillilans, were original members of the community and came over from Scotland. 'The largest holders of land were the Adairs, Agnews, Fergusons, Gillilans [*sic*] . . .' Lady Ferguson, *Sir Samuel Ferguson*, 1, p. 3.
27. *The Variorum Edition of the Poems of W. B. Yeats*, p. 416.

28. *Ibid.*, p. 409.
29. Samuel Ferguson, 'Willy Gilliland: An Ulster Ballad', p. 112.
30. *Ibid.*, p. 115.
31. *Ibid.*, p. 118.
32. *Ibid.*, p. 117.
33. *The Variorum Edition of the Poems of W. B. Yeats*, p. 347.
34. *Ibid.*, p. 347.
35. *Ibid.*, p. 414.
36. *Ibid.*, p. 416.
37. *Ibid., p. 348.*
38. *Ibid.*, p. 414.
39. Samuel Ferguson, 'Willy Gilliland: An Ulster Ballad', p. 112.
40. *Ibid.*, p. 113.
41. *Ibid.*, p. 118.
42. *The Variorum Edition of the Poems of W. B. Yeats*, p. 347.
43. *Ibid.*, p. 414.
44. *Ibid.*, p. 416.
45. Samuel Ferguson, 'Willy Gilliland: An Ulster Ballad', p. 112.
46. *Ibid.*, p. 116.
47. *The Variorum Edition of the Poems of W. B. Yeats*, pp. 374, 376.
48. *Ibid.*, p. 405.
49. *Ibid.*, p. 414.
50. *Ibid.*, p. 328.
51. *Uncollected Prose by W. B. Yeats*, I, p. 82.

All Souls' nights: Yeats, Sassoon and the dead

THOMAS MALLON

Nearing the end of his life, and approaching his final willingness to lie down in 'the foul rag-and-bone shop of the heart', Yeats filled his poetry with a receptiveness towards existence which led to both the energy of the 'old man' poems and the wise calm of 'Lapis Lazuli'. That poem tells us that real artists and builders

> know that Hamlet and Lear are gay;
> Gaiety transfiguring all that dread.
> All men have aimed at, found and lost;
> Black out; Heaven blazing into the head:
> Tragedy wrought to its uttermost.
> Though Hamlet rambles and Lear rages,
> And all the drop-scenes drop at once
> Upon a hundred thousand stages,
> It cannot grow by an inch or an ounce.[1]

If one poet can anticipate the utterance of another to the extent that he is able to offer a detailed refutation of it years before it is formulated – a time-bending notion that would have appealed to Yeats – then Siegfried Sassoon's 'The Facts', written in 1932, can stand as an almost uncanny rebuttal to the gaiety of 'Lapis Lazuli', which would not reach paper for six more years:

> Can a man face the facts of life and laugh? . . .
> Swift faced them and died mad, deaf and diseased.
> Shakespeare spoke out, went home, and wrote no more.
> Oblivion was the only epitaph
> They asked, as private persons, having eased
> Their spirits of the burden that they bore.
>
> The facts of life are fierce. One feels a wraith
> When facing them with luminous lyric faith.
> Daring to look within us, we discern

85

> The jungle. To the jungle we return
> More easily than most of us admit.
> In this thought-riddled twentieth-century day
> I cannot read – say 'Gulliver' – and feel gay,
> Or share – in 'Lear' – the pleasure of the Pit.[2]

Gaiety here is not 'transfiguring'; it is simply impossible.

This apparent inability to welcome the tragic emotion, or at least to realize tragedy's merciful limits, may seem to a reader only one more reason for him to think of Sassoon and Yeats as discrete literary quantities. Certainly there are great contrasts which do not invite easy association of one with the other: Yeats, a key figure and influence in 'modernism'; Sassoon, content to work within traditional poetic forms; Yeats, despite his fear of civil war, lending his poetic voice to the Irish rebellion; Sassoon, despite his anti-war poetry, essentially a good soldier who retreats into most of the Tory values of the country squire; Yeats, the vigorous mystic of Theosophism, gyres, *A Vision* and automatic writing; Sassoon, the seemingly quiet convert, late in life, to Roman Catholicism. And yet, in spite of these contrasts, and because some of them have been overstated, there are enough temperamental similarities between the poets to make a simultaneous reading of their poems instructive.

No matter how different the methods and styles of their searches, both men shared the spirit of the long quester after faith, certainty and system. Richard Ellmann has sensitively described the character of Yeats's search:

He labored a great deal to change his terms of reference from scepticism and superstition to knowledge and faith. He hoped to reconcile 'spiritist fact with credible philosophy'. The séance room must be made into a scientific laboratory; what he had learned in the back alleys of culture must be shown to be fundamentally what the greatest philosophers and religious men had always said. He never gave up hope of bringing together myth and fact into a new religion, or, as he called it, a new 'sacred drama' of Unity of Being.[3]

Michael Thorpe, Sassoon's most important commentator, has outlined that poet's reaching after faith in a way which shows it to have been less daring, and less spectacularly synthetic, than Yeats's, but possessed of the same duration and seriousness:

so scrupulous is the search that it issues in no firm belief until more than thirty years have passed . . . The transitions from a wish to believe, to hope, to positive belief are gradual: belief comes with the slow inevitability of organic growth, not in a passion of conversion.[4]

Even if, however, Sassoon's ultimate conversion had an inevitable, or 'organic', quality, it was fought for deliberately – inside the mind. His was an 'Elected Silence':

> Where voices vanish into dream,
>   I have discovered, from the pride
> Of temporal trophydoms, this theme,
>   That silence is the ultimate guide.
>
> Allow me now much musing-space
>   To shape my secrecies alone . . .[5]

His house in Heytesbury became, often in the hours of night, what Yeats's Ballylee castle was to him – a spiritual meeting place for his past and present, belief and doubt, conscious and unconscious selves, a place where they could attempt to join themselves into a final and orderly faith.

Both Sassoon and Yeats were affected by the emotional pull of the past, a desire for solitude, a belief in ghosts, and the need to have 'consultations' with the dead – often their old friends – as they sought answers to spiritual questions. The gradualness and the doctrinal conclusion of Sassoon's spiritual search have obscured the fact that it shared a mystical tendency with Yeats's nocturnal reachings after faith. Sassoon's friend, Dame Felicitas Corrigan, a spiritual advisor in his later years, has written of the importance of angels in his religious vision:

They convey the sense of the divine, speak as oracles of God, and with their powerful intervention in human affairs, they minister to man. Sassoon was a Jew. His angels may very well have been housed in that uncharitable element, his inherited subconscious mind which, he was fond of asserting, knew a lot more than the

conscious one. Within a minute of turning the light out, visualiza-
tions of angels as well as of automatic writing and oriental
architecture often accompanied his falling asleep.[6]

These Byzantine visions of the subconscious would invite the
description 'Yeatsian' even if Yeats were not the other half of
the comparison being undertaken here. They are the pro-
ducts of a mind, like Yeats's, which was convinced of the
constant influence of past ages and dead persons upon its
continuing growth, understanding and reception of revelation.

Called by Eliot 'pre-eminently the poet of middle age',
Yeats was possessed of a temperament which was inherently
elegiac.[7] A sense of the past as being more graceful and even
imaginatively significant than the present was a characteristic
of mind he shared with Sassoon. The one shaken by the
violence of a revolution he at first welcomed and then
recoiled from, the other scarred by mechanized war, both
poets reacted against the present in a 'political' way, but that
reaction was abetted by a fundamental, even instinctive,
nostalgia. By an 'October twilight' in 1916, Yeats has already
counted the swans at Coole nineteen times, and his 'heart is
sore' with a sense of impending loss:

> Among what rushes will they build,
> By what lake's edge or pool
> Delight men's eyes when I awake some day
> To find they have flown away.[8]

The nineteen completed countings of present swans provide
no reassurance; instead, they are a sign of anxiety in a man for
whom 'All's changed . . .'[9] Sassoon's early sonnet 'October'
takes similarly small comfort from that month's familiar
russet scene. The voice in the sestet tries to provide some of
Shelley's 'West Wind' confidence in the future, in the face of
winter's approach, but focus and emotion remain held by the
past, refusing to jump ahead a season. It is a past spring he
thinks of:

> Now do ye dream of Spring when greening shaws
> Confer with the shrewd breezes, and of slopes

> Flower-kirtled, and of April, virgin guest;
> Days that ye love, despite their windy flaws,
> Since they are woven with all joys and hopes
> Whereof ye nevermore shall be possessed.[10]

It is this same spirit which will many years later prompt Sassoon to see that

> consolement deepeningly depends
> On hoarded time, enriched and redesigned.
> So is it with us all. And thus we find
> Endeared survivals that our thought defends.[11]

Both poets lament the decline of courtesy, grace and order, and they look towards women and great houses as embodiments of those values. In 'Upon a Dying Lady', Yeats marvels that his subject 'has not grown uncivil', and eulogizes 'the old distinguished grace' she represents.[12] Sassoon's 'To an Old Lady Dead' asserts that its subject's 'earth-success' was that she lived her 'life in grove and garden shady / Of social Academe, good talk and taste'.[13] Yeats's 'House Shaken by the Land Agitation' owes some of its 'eagle thoughts' to the fact that in it 'wings have memory of wings'; the present owes any grandeur it has to the past.[14] Sassoon's 'Monody on the Demolition of Devonshire House', even with its sprightly satiric gait, manages to mourn eloquently 'wintry strange / Frontage of houses raw-ly-lit by change'.[15] His involvement with past landscape may be sometimes less imaginatively intense than Yeats's – 'In Heytesbury Wood' rather blandly looks back to a ' "well-ordered distant mid-Victorian time" ' – but the willingness to be carried back by the signs of other times is shared.[16]

Their most important common ground, however, is their sense of the influence of the dead, especially those departed whom they knew in life. Yeats's loyalty to 'the last romantics' and his insistence that his glory was he had 'such friends', the memories of whom are the most '[b]eautiful lofty things' he possesses, are as well known as anything in his poems. Sassoon's poetry is even more frequently preoccupied with past presences. A man's 'Progressions', he tells us, build

> A mind, matured in wearying bones, returning slowly
> Toward years revisioned richly while fruitions fail him, –
> A mind, renouncing hopes and finding lost loves holy.[17]

Like violin music, bright portraits and matured wine, 'Dead friends pervade the gloom' he is subject to.[18]

This sense of the holy influence of the dead combines with the emotional pull of past places and atmospheres to make possible, and frequent, in both poets' work, the literal presences of ghosts. Yeats's ghosts are, of course, only one part of his startling cosmogony, but he was attracted and tormented by the idea of their existence and the possibilities of their mission:

> Ah! when the ghost begins to quicken,
> Confusion of the death-bed over, is it sent
> Out naked on the roads, as the books say, and stricken
> By the injustice of the skies for punishment?[19]

In his note to 'An Image from a Past Life', in which the 'She' declares herself 'afraid / Of the hovering thing night brought [her]', Yeats theorized that it is not images of actual past persons and things that appear to us in dreams, but rather universalized modifications of them from *Spiritus Mundi* and other extra-conscious sources.[20] But the ghosts who visited Yeats in his poetry were far less Platonic and far more palpable than those which live in more than one mind. Robert Gregory, Alfred Pollexfen, MacGregor Mathers and others are actual friends remembered, presences available to be summoned. Readers travelling in Yeats's spiritual galaxy come to know his ghosts as real creatures, men and women out of one man's past.

Ghosts in Sassoon's poems appear with sometimes even more substance than those in Yeats's. Sassoon had seen dead men, many of them, lying recently and horribly so in the trenches, and they sometimes returned to him still attached, in agony, to their bodies:

> The darkness of their dying
> Grows one with War recorded;
> Whose swindled ghosts are crying
> From shell-holes in the past,
> *Our deeds with lies were lauded,*
> *Our bones with wrongs rewarded.*
> Dream voices these – denying
> Dud laurels to the last.[21]

Other ghosts return to Sassoon less tormented, but no less forcefully. The assurance he gives 'To an Eighteenth Century Poet' that his lines, when read, bring him back to life, is not a banality on the immortality of verse, but a serious meditation upon 'how terrestrial existence / Plays tricks with death'.[22] The influence of the dead's 'Vibrations' is keen and thorough:

> Caught unaware in day-dream silences,
> I hear you, vanished voices, where such peace
> Imbues my being as when your gladness breathed;
> And now like leafy whispering it is,
> And now slow shadows of the towering trees
> On lawns that your experience has bequeathed.[23]

He knows that the wisdom of the world advises '[t]o keep no faith with ghostly friends', but he breaks this taboo with earnest deliberation.[24] He asks the dead:

> How can you be believed in, how made certain,
> How sought beyond the silences of learning?
> And how, revisitants by life envisioned,
> Can what we are empower your quiet returning?[25]

Even when the ghosts 'mock and stultify', he cannot disperse their existence and influence:

> Dawn comes and re-creates the sleepless room;
> And eyesight asks what arguing plagues exist.
> But in that garret of uneasy gloom
> Which is your brain, the presences persist.[26]

And it is rarely dispersal that is wanted. As he grows older, he in fact regrets the diminishing of his powers to conjure the ghosts, with their wisdom and inspiration, quite as tangibly as before. In 'Solitudes at Sixty', he records:

> Beloved or valued ghosts, these reappear
> At my peculiar prompting. Known by heart,
> Finite impersonations, learnt by ear,
> Their voices talk in character and depart.
>
> They, once my wise and faithful, have no being:
> No supersensual agency can bring
> Those presences from silence and unseeing:
> They dwell secure from world's importuning.[27]

Neither poet fled his ghosts – not even when they arrived as terrifyingly as *'a coat upon a coat-hanger'*.[28]

Both poets sought the dead often enough to learn that certain atmospheres and hours were more likely to give up ghosts than others; as a consequence, many 'midnight interiors' became the settings of their poems. Midnight, in Yeats's work, is often marked by careful arrangement of what his Ribh dismissed as 'mental furniture', the summoning of memories and ghosts, in order that the soul better understand its journey and purpose.[29] The hour is one of preparation for intense meditation. In the second section ('My House') of 'Meditations in Time of Civil War', Yeats imagines *'Il Penseroso's* Platonist' at his contemplative work:

> Benighted travellers
> From markets and fairs
> Have seen his midnight candle glimmering.[30]

The hour is somewhat earlier, but the meditation conducted in 'The Tower' begins with the poet asking for the dead. He will invoke

> Images and memories
> From ruin or from ancient trees,
> For [he] would ask a question of them all.[31]

These presences can become, as darkness grows, even stronger than the living:

> Let the new faces play what tricks they will
> In the old rooms; night can outbalance day,
> Our shadows rove the garden gravel still,
> The living seem more shadowy than they.[32]

It is at midnight that the poet sets his table for ghosts in preparation for a solitary's séance:

> Midnight has come, and the great Christ Church Bell
> And many a lesser bell sound through the room;
> And it is All Souls' Night,
> And two long glasses brimmed with muscatel
> Bubble upon the table. A ghost may come . . .[33]

Sassoon's summonings of the dead were also conducted alone in his rooms in the late hours. More consistently reclusive than Yeats, from his 'somewhat segregated' childhood on,[34] he described, in one of his war poems, this inclination of his temperament:

> I dream of a small firelit room
> With yellow candles burning straight,
> And kindly books that hold me late.[35]

These rooms may come alive with his own ghosts: 'Sleep-walkers empty-eyed come strangely down the stairs. / These are my selves'.[36] These may trouble him, but the ghosts of others come to his room as well, and they are usually benevolent spirits. When he writes about his house in a manner akin to Yeats's civil war meditation, he addresses it these words:

>   I can feel
> That when your ghosts revisit you they steal
> From room to room like moonlight long ago:
> And if some voice from silence haunts my head
> I only wonder who it was that said –
> 'House, I am here because I loved you so'.[37]

Even when he can imagine the nocturnal influence of darker spirits, it is only their 'frustrated spells' he envisions.[38]

Sassoon has often been compared to Vaughan, whose quiet intelligence was granted such spectacular visions, and whom he admired and envied. At Vaughan's grave he thought of that poet's 'skull that housed white angels and had vision / Of daybreak through the gateways of the mind'.[39] But Sassoon's visions were less overwhelming. In 'A Midnight Interior' he shows how his quest for spiritual revelation is a

more deliberate one than Vaughan's. He describes what he
sees in a light shining late in his room; his envisionings are
not part of a white light suddenly ablaze for an eternal
expanse, as Vaughan's can be, but rather things carefully
sought in the small circle cast by a man-made lamp:

> To-night while I was pondering in my chair
> I saw for the first time a circle of brightness
> Made by my patient lamp up on the ceiling.
> It shone like a strange flower; and then my stare
> Discovered an arctic snowstorm in that whiteness;
> And then some pastoral vale of rayed revealing.[40]

He is humbly aware that his own spiritual capacities are less
literally flashing than Vaughan's, but he is willing to conduct
his painstaking night-time vigils to see what he can. As he
describes himself in one of his 'Brevities':

> I am the man who with a luminous look
> Sits up at night to write a ruminant book.[41]

Like Yeats, he sets a sort of midnight table for the dead, the
spirits of his friends who have 'all gone into the world of
light'.

What is wanted from these spirits? Why do the poets seek
them? To put it simply, as models of earthly conduct and for
knowledge of a world beyond the body's present one. In
'Blood and the Moon', written at Thoor Ballylee, Yeats
declared that 'wisdom is the property of the dead, / A
something incompatible with life'.[42] His elegy for Robert
Gregory began as a meditation on more than one dead man:

> Discoverers of forgotten truth
> Or mere companions of my youth,
> All, all are in my thoughts to-night being dead.

Lionel Johnson, Synge and the astrologist George Pollexfen
are called up for their intellects and passions; but the memory
of Gregory, 'Our Sidney', eliminates the need for all the
others. His memory, by itself, brings all the virtues the poet
had set out to remember. But here it is not really Gregory's
ghost the poet is perceiving; it is simply his memory – there
is no apparition. The poem ends in sadness; death remains

intractable, something that has taken the poet's 'heart for speech'.[43] This poem, for all its beauty, remains less spiritually capacious than the magnificent 'All Souls' Night' of a few years later – the poem that would serve as the epilogue to Yeats's *Vision*. Here Yeats does not merely ponder the memories of his dead friends; he sets out a goblet for their very ghosts. He does not think of their lives and virtues merely as a guide for living; rather, he calls upon them for spiritual communion. The ghosts provide a mental and poetic excitement that mere memory could not. Yeats has his own 'mummy truths' to tell them, truths '[w]hereat the living mock'. The ghosts he calls – William Thomas Horton, Florence Emery and MacGregor Mathers – are all fellow mystics and occultists. The sadness of 'Robert Gregory' gives way to a gay, even playful, confidence. In calling up Mathers, the poet thinks:

> A ghost-lover he was
> And may have grown more arrogant being a ghost.

'All Souls' Night' is Yeats in full spiritual flight. Praising single-minded vision in spite of its pains and risks, he is on his way to achieving, like Florence Emery, a soul 'free and yet fast'. But the ghosts remain a source of advanced wisdom and reason for envy as they take an 'ecstasy' from the fumes that '[n]o living man can drink from the whole wine'. He is not using All Souls' night as the church would have it (and as Sassoon himself would use it in his poem 'All Souls' Day'), to pray for souls suffering in purgatory, but rather to infect himself with the spiritual 'delight' of ghost-believers now themselves made ghosts.[44] As Harold Bloom has written:

All Souls' Night deprecates the sober ear and the outward eye, and celebrates the dead who in their lives were drunk with vision, as Yeats chooses (here) to see himself as being. In death the questers have found their element, and drink from the whole wine of their gnosis. Yeats, a living man, is blind and drinks his drop, but is half contented to be blind, whether to the faults of the dead or of the full vision awaiting him in the whole wine of his own death, when his glance and thought alike will be fulfilled.[45]

Sassoon's ghosts often appeared to him with a purpose that seemed mysterious, but if he could not always discern the exact cause for their coming, he knew that they were connected with the difficult spiritual journey he was making. Ghosts were 'Presences Perfected' who indicated a triumph of the spirit if not an exact prescription for his own:

> I saw them. Numberless they stood
> Half-way toward heaven, that men might mark
> The grandeur of their ghostlihood
> Burning divinely on the dark.[46]

The 'Revisitation' of the spirit of his teacher, Dr W. H. R. Rivers (author of *Instinct and the Unconscious*), is marked by some uncertainty. He is sure of Rivers's survival and continuing influence, but there is a lack of exactness about the ghost's shape and immediate mission:

> What voice revisits me this night? What face
> To my heart's room returns?
> From that perpetual silence where the grace
> Of human sainthood burns
> Hastes he once more to harmonize and heal?
> I know not. Only I feel
> His influence undiminished.
> And his life's work, in me and many, unfinished.[47]

Another late night 'Visitant' also fails to make exact identity and purpose known:

> Someone else invades me for an hour or two.
> Clocked occluded self wrote never lines like his.
> Me he has no need of. And I know not who
> Or from what irrational inwardness he is.[48]

He eventually realizes, as his spirit blooms toward its final religious happiness, that these presences are beckoning him to their world, one beyond his own. In 'Human Bondage' he asserts:

> I know a night of stars within me;
> Through eyes of dream I have perceived
> Blest apparitions who would win me
> Home to what innocence believed.

But as yet he remains a 'blithe structure of sensation, / Prisoned and impassioned by [his] clay.'[49] The time comes, however, when spiritual certainty arrives as 'A Chord', and he is capable of flights unfettered by the flesh:

> On stillness came a chord,
> While I, the instrument,
> Knew long-withheld reward . . .[50]

The ghosts had been intimations of what he perceived as this ultimate grace and truth. He meets them finally on terms of joy similar to Yeats's in 'All Souls' Night', however different the theological architecture of each man's conception of the afterlife.

Byron imagined friendship as 'Love without his wings'. But in the poems of Yeats and Sassoon friends become ghosts, and the ghosts exert an influence that eventually leads each poet to soar towards revelation. It is a particular feature of temperament, this eagerness to conjure and make use of spirits, and it unites two poets otherwise so different – one apparently so very 'Irish', with all the mysticism of the stereotype, the other so very 'English', a fox-hunting man out of a print by Bewick. However separated by culture, generation and personality, each man held his own séance, asking for news of another country and receiving a message that amazed him into poetry.

1. *The Variorum Edition of the Poems of W. B. Yeats*, ed. Peter Allt and Russell K. Alspach (New York, 1957), pp. 565–6. (All further citations from Yeats's poems are from this edition, hereafter designated *Poems of W. B. Yeats*.)

2. Siegfried Sassoon, *Collected Poems, 1908–1956* (London, 1961), p. 171. (All subsequent citations from Sassoon's poems are from this edition, hereafter designated *Collected Poems*.)

3. Richard Ellmann, *Yeats: The Man and the Masks* (New York, 1948), p. 291.

4. Michael Thorpe, *Siegfried Sassoon: A Critical Study* (London, 1967), p. 208.

5. 'Elected Silence', *Collected Poems*, p. 210.

6. Dame Felicitas Corrigan, *Siegfried Sassoon: Poet's Pilgrimage* (London, 1973), pp. 28–9.

7. T. S. Eliot, 'Yeats', in *On Poetry and Poets* (New York, 1961), p. 301.
8. 'The Wild Swans at Coole', *Poems of W. B. Yeats*, pp. 322–3.
9. *Ibid.*
10. 'October', *Collected Poems*, p. 52.
11. 'Ultimate Values', *Collected Poems*, p. 277.
12. 'Upon a Dying Lady', *Poems of W. B. Yeats*, pp. 362 and 365.
13. 'To an Old Lady Dead', *Collected Poems*, p. 184.
14. 'Upon a House Shaken by the Land Agitation', *Poems of W. B. Yeats*, p. 264.
15. 'Monody on the Demolition of Devonshire House', *Collected Poems*, p. 131.
16. 'In Heytesbury Wood', *Collected Poems*, p. 234.
17. 'Progressions', *Collected Poems*, p. 254.
18. 'Old Music', *Collected Poems*, p. 255.
19. 'The Cold Heaven', *Poems of W. B. Yeats*, p. 316.
20. 'An Image from a Past Life', *Poems of W. B. Yeats*, p. 390 and note on pp. 821–3.
21. 'Ex-Service', *Collected Poems*, p. 217.
22. 'To an Eighteenth Century Poet', *Collected Poems*, p. 183.
23. 'Vibrations', *Collected Poems*, p. 219.
24. 'The wisdom of the world is this', *Collected Poems*, p. 194.
25. 'Again the dead, the dead again demanding', *Collected Poems*, p. 220.
26. 'Break silence. You have listened overlong', *Collected Poems*, p. 217.
27. 'Solitudes at Sixty', *Collected Poems*, p. 276.
28. 'The Apparitions', *Poems of W. B. Yeats*, p. 624.
29. 'Ribh Considers Christian Love Insufficient', *Poems of W. B. Yeats*, p. 558.
30. 'Meditations in Time of Civil War', *Poems of W. B. Yeats*, pp. 419–420.
31. 'The Tower', *Poems of W. B. Yeats*, p. 410.
32. 'The New Faces', *Poems of W. B. Yeats*, p. 435.
33. 'All Souls' Night', *Poems of W. B. Yeats*, p. 470.
34. Sassoon, *The Old Century and Seven More Years* (New York, 1938), p. 157.
35. 'When I'm Among a Blaze of Lights', *Collected Poems*, p. 14.
36. 'My past has gone to bed, Upstairs in clockless rooms', *Collected Poems*, p. 213.
37. 'Eulogy of My House', *Collected Poems*, p. 233.
38. 'While Reading a Ghost Story', *Collected Poems*, p. 235.
39. 'At the Grave of Henry Vaughan', *Collected Poems*, p. 190.
40. 'A Midnight Interior', *Collected Poems*, p. 190.
41. 'Brevities', *Collected Poems*, p. 231.

42. 'Blood and the Moon', *Poems of W. B. Yeats*, p. 482.
43. 'In Memory of Major Robert Gregory', *Poems of W. B. Yeats*, p. 324.
44. 'All Souls' Night', *Poems of W. B. Yeats*, pp. 472–4.
45. Harold Bloom, *Yeats* (New York, 1970), p. 370.
46. 'Presences Perfected', *Collected Poems*, p. 227.
47. 'Revisitation', *Collected Poems*, p. 221.
48. 'The Visitant', *Collected Poems*, p. 292.
49. 'Human Bondage', *Collected Poems*, p. 300.
50. 'A Chord', *Collected Poems*, p. 303.

James Joyce, Patrick Pearse and the theme of execution

JEANNE A. FLOOD

As the last line of print in *Ulysses* notes, Joyce wrote the novel between 1914 and 1921 in Trieste, Zurich, and Paris. Precisely in this period, politics in Ireland were in a continuously volatile and ultimately revolutionary condition. In 1925, Valery Larbaud noted how appropriate it was that his pre-publication *conférence* on *Ulysses* was given on 7 December 1921, within hours of the newspaper announcement of the signing of the Anglo-Irish treaty.[1] This recognition of a link between *Ulysses* and the revolution in Irish politics which occurred while it was being written had also been made in the first months of the existence of the new Irish state when Desmond Fitzgerald, one of its ministers, tried to associate Joyce's work with the state in an international forum. Fitzgerald had served with the rebels in the Post Office in 1916 and had subscribed to *Ulysses* in 1921.[2] In March of 1922, as Minister for Publicity, he visited Joyce in Paris and announced that he had proposed that the Irish cabinet nominate Joyce for the Nobel Prize.[3] Though nothing came of Fitzgerald's gesture, the fact that it was made indicates recognition by one actually involved in the revolution of the special status of *Ulysses* in relation to the new state. Desmond Ryan, the author of an important eye-witness account of the Easter Rising, in his eloquent memoir of his life in revolutionary Ireland wrote of *Ulysses*: 'It alone would explain the Irish revolution, for it reveals Dublin as none other than an Irishman could reveal her, an Irishman who at heart loves Dublin, and writes with all the indignation of love, the very pulse of this remorseless and brutal protest.'[4]

In spite of the early recognition of a relationship between *Ulysses* and revolutionary political change in Ireland, critics have generally shown little interest in exploring that connection. Probably because of its 1904 time setting, *Ulysses* is not presented as a relevant text in such studies of literature and the Irish revolution as William Irwin Thompson's *The Imagination of an Insurrection* (New York, 1967) and Peter Costello's *The Heart Grown Brutal* (Dublin, 1977). Relatively few critics of Joyce have been interested in Irish history. Helene Cixous in *The Exile of James Joyce* (New York, 1972) is one of the exceptions. Her book is an attempt to consider the politics and culture of Ireland in relation to Joyce's work, but the simplified and impressionistic approach Cixous has taken toward Irish historical events severely limits the book's effectiveness. Bernard Benstock's *James Joyce: The Undiscovered Country* (Dublin, 1977) is an exploration of Irish political themes in Joyce's work, but Benstock is interested in politics in Ireland only in so far as it constitutes an element in Joyce's fiction. Unlike Cixous and Benstock, Richard Ellmann and John Garvin look at Joyce's work in the context of Irish political history. Ellmann in *The Consciousness of Joyce* (New York, 1977) notes that *Ulysses* was written during the Irish revolution and holds that Joyce consciously intended the book to express sympathy for Arthur Griffith and the ideal of Sinn Fein. Garvin in *James Joyce's Disunited Kingdom* (Dublin, 1976) argues that Joyce had a strong interest in political events in Ireland throughout his life. By analysis of specific allusions in *Ulysses* and especially in *Finnegans Wake*, he makes an impressive case for recognition of the interplay between what he calls 'the Irish dimension' and Joyce's major works. The present essay, like the work of these critics, is intended to suggest a relationship between Irish historical events and Joyce's work. It attempts to build this relationship upon a comparison of the treatment of a specific theme as it appears in the speeches and writing of Patrick Pearse and in *Ulysses*. The approach here differs from the work of Cixous and Benstock in that it views Joyce's work in the context of Irish politics and culture rather than considering Irish issues simply as themes in Joyce's work. Where Ellmann and Garvin are concerned with specific and conscious attitudes toward Irish politics that Joyce expressed in his fiction, I want to suggest a relationship between *Ulysses* and political change in Ireland that does not arise from his conscious opinion of events occurring in Ireland while he was writing the book.

It is my contention that *Ulysses* is related to revolutionary Irish politics because, as Desmond Ryan understood, the novel and the revolution came out of an identical experience of Irish life. Joyce himself had a strong sense of having been shaped by the historical experience of Ireland. In 1919, when guerilla war was raging in Ireland and Joyce was at work on 'Cyclops' in Zurich, Frank Budgen remarked to him that the current Anglo-Irish strife would be resolved if England simply granted political autonomy to Ireland. Joyce replied that he did not want such a change in the status of Ireland to occur: ' "Ireland is what she is, . . . and therefore I am what I am because of the relations that have existed between England and Ireland. Tell me why you think I ought to wish to change the conditions that gave Ireland and me a shape and a destiny?" '[5] The context of Joyce's answer suggests that he saw the shape and destiny of Ireland to be a condition of never resolved struggle for separation from England and himself as a man whose personal destiny was the heroic expression of a self marked and imprinted by struggling Ireland. Joyce's remark to Budgen is a variation on that made by Stephen Dedalus to the ardent nationalist, Davin, in *A Portrait of the Artist as a Young Man*: ' – This race and this country and this life produced me . . . I shall express myself as I am.'[6] It is significant that the statements of both Joyce and Stephen occur in conversations which relate to political change in Ireland This conviction that the shape of his being is determined by the historical experience of Ireland is the basis on which I wish to suggest the relationship between Joyce's novel and Irish political life. It is through his experience of himself as the person he is that Irish politics and Irish history enter Joyce's consciousness and his work.

As an Irish Catholic living through the historical experience of his place and his era, Joyce was affected by the same forces that worked upon other Irishmen, who were fellow Catholics and possessed of a sense of Ireland as a national entity ambiguously bound to another state. This shared sense of Irish history united Joyce to these men, and them to him and to each other. Joyce was divided from the race, country, and life which produced him not by the demonstrably nationalist sense of Irish historical experience which he felt to be part of himself, but by his attitude toward that sense of Irish history. Joyce's exile and his commitment to the work of the artist, central concerns in all of his novels, constitute an extreme response to his culture's vision of the Irish past which should be related to another extreme response, the death by execution of Patrick Pearse, the provisional President of the Irish Republic and the commander of the insurrectionary forces during Easter Week.

By a process only now being explored, Pearse became the paradigmatic figure of the Rising.[7] Through his posthumously published writings and through the influence of his thought on popular and academic historiography, he was also the authoritative interpreter of the significance of the Rising to his own contemporaries and to successive generations of Irishmen.[8] Pearse's concept of Ireland and its demands on Irishmen, validated by his execution, mobilized powerful social and cultural forces and ultimately worked to effect revolutionary change. Although Joyce the artist and Pearse the patriot-martyr were not direct influences on one another, both shared an identical experience of Ireland and of themselves as Irishmen. Both Joyce and Pearse felt Ireland's claim on them to be overwhelming; both envisioned that claim with precisely the same imagery. Pearse enacted that imagery in his own life, and Joyce expressed it in the writing of *Ulysses*. The central effort of this study is to show that both Joyce and Pearse saw the process by which Ireland was to be definitively separated from England as so drastic that they could not survive it. Further, they both experienced the certainty of their own destruction in the cataclysm in which Ireland would separate from England through the same psychic representation, that is through an image of fusion of son and mother into one figure. Both Joyce's novel and Pearse's political actions are matters of the greatest complexity. The attempt to show that they are related to each other will demand a certain limitation of focus on both, which should not be seen as a crudely reductionist view of either.

The lives of Pearse and Joyce converge in interesting ways. They grew up in the same city at the same time; there was less than three years' difference in their ages. They were both Catholic, and both middle-class, though the Pearses were rising and the Joyces declining. They were enrolled at the Royal University at the same time. Not surprisingly, they knew each other. Joyce told Frank Budgen that during the period in which he studied Irish under the auspices of the Gaelic League, Pearse was his teacher.[9] The character of Hughes, the Irish teacher in *Stephen Hero*, seems based in large part on Pearse.[10] Repeatedly we see that Joyce and Pearse responded to the same cultural issues, though in every case the cherished enthusiasms of Pearse were the ardent antipathies of Joyce. For example, in 1898, the nineteen-year-old Pearse published a monograph, *Three Lectures on Gaelic Topics*,[11] which is devoted to the praise of the Irish language and of the saga and folk literature which it produced. In 1901, the nineteen-year-old Joyce published *The Day of the Rabblement* to attack the Irish Literary Theatre for contemplating the production of one play in Irish and another based on one of the Irish sagas.[12] Pearse found the Ulster cycle 'the finest epic stuff in the world . . . the story . . . greater than any Greek story, . . . the theme . . . as great as Milton's.'[13] Stephen Dedalus refers to Irish saga material as 'the myth upon which no individual mind had ever drawn out a line of beauty'.[14] In the Irish-speaking peasants of the West, Pearse found the well-spring of a renewed national life,[15] and Joyce found, at least in Lady Gregory's presentation of it, 'a land almost fabulous in its sorrow and senility'.[16] Joyce and Pearse responded to the nationalist themes of the language, the Gaelic past, and the peasantry in exactly opposed ways. Also in opposite ways, they articulate an issue which is more complicated and more deeply enmeshed in their personal lives. For both of them, the claims of Ireland were ultimately maternal and religious in nature. Each placed in a central position in his own work his own relation to his mother, which each linked to the church and to death in the nationalist cause.

Joyce built *A Portrait of the Artist as a Young Man* on his own rejection of mother/Ireland/church. In the final chapter of the novel, Stephen's idea of freedom for the Irishman is worked out in a metaphor of escape from maternal entrapment when he speaks to Davin, who has just remarked that their generation, like the generations of the past, will have the chance to die for Ireland: ' – The soul is born, he said vaguely, first in those moments I told you of. It has a slow and dark birth, more mysterious than the birth of the body. When the soul of a man is born in this country there are nets flung at it to hold it back from flight. You talk to me of nationality, language, religion. I shall try to fly by those nets' (p. 203). In Joyce's metaphor, the instant of birth offers the possibility of freedom, conceptualized as flight. But freedom is menaced by the matrix which has generated the person. The metaphor identifies the culture of nationalist Ireland with the mother, and it presents the mother as the child's destruction at the moment of its birth. The terrible implications of the image of the newly-born trapped against the body from which it has just separated are intensified when Stephen closes the conversation with the famous statement which presents Ireland as the cannibal mother, 'the old sow that eats her farrow' (p. 203).

For Pearse too the maternal theme is centrally associated with Ireland. In his literary writing he presents and glorifies the figure of the mother who sends her sons to die for Ireland. One of these heroic women speaks in a 1915 poem, which is called 'The Mother'.

> I do not grudge them: Lord, I do not grudge
> My two strong sons that I have seen go out
> To break their strength and die, they and a few,
> In bloody protest for a glorious thing,
> They shall be spoken of among their people,

The generations shall remember them,
And call them blessed.[17]

As happens often when Pearse turns to aesthetic rather than polemical expression, the language of the poem is deadened, inadequate to the emotion of the situation. The one element in the poem that achieves more than minimal expressiveness is the echo in the last two lines quoted of the words the pregnant Mary spoke to Elizabeth in the Magnificat (Luke 1. 46–55). Clearly one function of this biblical resonance is to identify as messianic the dead or dying sons. But the echo also associates the pregnancy of Mary with the desolate condition of the speaker of the poem. Thus Pearse collapses into one moment the pregnancy of the mother and her calm contemplation of the death of her sons in the sacred battle. They separate from her only to die in the fight for Ireland. Pearse and Joyce work with precisely the same set of associations to the maternal when they present Ireland as mother. They converge on the moment of birth, and for both of them, the destruction of the child is involved with his bond to the mother. Pearse sees as heroic that which horrifies Joyce. Pearse's *mater dolorosa* and Joyce's murderous sow are the antithetical variations on the same image of mother/ Ireland/church.

Recently revisionist Irish historians, such as F. X. Martin and Francis Shaw, have pointed out the deliberateness with which Pearse set about creating a personal legend which would identify him as the heroic martyr in the cause of Irish freedom.[18] A significant element in that legend is his presentation of his mother and her family in relation to his own life. At some point, probably in the last two years of his life, Pearse wrote the first five chapters of an autobiography.[19] In its opening chapter, 'Myself – My Father – My Mother and Her People', he devotes only one paragraph to his father. James Pearse, an Englishman, was a stone worker who merely drifted to Ireland; however, writes his son, 'through his children, his name was to become an Irish name' (p. 16). The chapter on ancestry, as its title indicates, concentrates on

Pearse's mother's family. He presents a genealogical summary linking himself to his maternal great-great grandfather,
Walter Brady, an Irish speaker and a rebel in the Rising of
1798: 'Margaret, daughter of Patrick, son of Walter, son of
Walter, was my mother' (p. 18). The autobiography shows
Pearse's childhood as an analogue of Christ's. Thus the
biological mother is married to an Englishman, but not really
married at all. Her son belongs solely to her people, and it is
through her son that her husband achieves Irish nationality.
Further, Pearse shows himself hailed at birth by an old
woman who reacted as Anna did when she saw the Christ
child in the temple. His maternal great-aunt, also named
Margaret, was present at Pearse's birth, 'and she has told me
how her heart leaped when it was found I was a boy' (p. 19).
The two maternal Margarets of the Brady family seem to
recognize in Pearse the revolutionary messiah.[20] Thus his
mother sang rebel songs to him in the cradle, and while he
recovered from an illness at age seven, Aunt Margaret told
him of Wolfe Tone and Robert Emmet and sang again the
laments and protests which had been the lullabies of his
infancy (p. 39). Pearse's autobiographical effort breaks off
with the suggestion that the work of his life is rooted in that
boyhood experience of sickness and passivity during which a
beloved maternal figure transmitted to him the rebel tradition and its obligations: 'That long convalescence is, in the
retrospect, the happiest and, at the same time, the most
important period in my life. In it, all the strengths and fealties
and right desires that have worked in me, and have given to
my life such utility as it can claim, have authentically their
roots' (p. 40).

For Pearse, the image of the boy as patriot and redeemer is
powerfully compelling. Besides appearing in his literary
work, most notably in the 1912 play, *The King*,[21] the
heroically doomed boy was a significant factor in the found-
ing in 1908 of St Enda's, Pearse's bilingual school for boys.
The school was formed on what Pearse thought to be the
model of the ancient Gaelic educational system, and he
intended the school to restore to Ireland the heroic and

sacrificial benefits of that system: 'We seek to recreate and perpetuate in Éire, the knightly tradition of the macradh of Eamhain Macha, dead at the ford "in the beauty of their boyhood." '[22] In his writing about St Enda's between 1908 and 1910, Pearse repeatedly connected Cuchulain and the slain boy-corps with Christ in the category of redemptive children. As time went on, he added to the group one more exhibit, the Irish boy rebel condemned to death, a figure ultimately associated with Robert Emmet. Though not a boy – he was twenty-five at his execution in 1803 – Emmet died the death that most attracted Pearse: 'Here at St Enda's we have tried to keep before us . . . that gesture of the head, that gallant smiling gesture, which has been an eternal gesture in Irish history; it was most memorably made by Emmet when he mounted the scaffold in Thomas Street, smiling, he who had left so much' (pp. 75–6).

The students at St Enda's were expected to restore to common use in Ireland 'that laughing gesture of a young man that is going into battle or climbing to a gibbet' (p. 76). In *An Macaomh* in 1913, Pearse as headmaster wrote an account of what he says was 'the only really vivid dream' he had ever had as an adult (p. 77). In the dream, a St Enda's pupil plays out a version of the Emmet execution scene: 'I dreamt that I saw a pupil of mine, one of our boys at St Enda's, standing alone upon a platform above a mighty sea of people; and I understood that he was about to die there for some august cause, Ireland's or another. He looked extraordinarily proud and joyous, lifting his head with a smile almost of amusement' (p. 76).

Although for Pearse boyhood is persistently associated with the idea of execution, and indeed with the whole task of revolution, he began in his thirties to enact his own identification with Robert Emmet. In 1910, he moved the school from its newly remodelled quarters in Dublin to suburban Rathfarnham, an area full of associations to Emmet. 'In truth, it was the spirit of Emmet that led me to these hillsides', he wrote after the school had been relocated (p. 54). The move lost Pearse half of the enrollment of St

Enda's and put him into financial difficulties from which he never recovered. But the losses were worth the gain: 'We know that Emmet walked under these trees . . . he must often have sat in this room where I now sit, and, lifting his eyes, have seen that mountain as I see it now' (pp. 55–6).

In the early part of 1914, Pearse came to the United States to raise money for the school. On 2 and 9 March in New York City, he gave two orations, both entitled 'Robert Emmet and the Ireland of Today'.[23] In both speeches, Pearse noted the immediate possibility of a Home Rule settlement on the one hand, and on the other, the presence of civilian armies on Irish soil. 'There is again in Ireland the murmur of a marching and talk of guns and tactics', he told the Americans, obviously exultant that a political settlement was steadily becoming more difficult (p. 73). Against the possibility of negotiated settlement with England, Pearse invoked the heroic suffering of the past, and most especially the death of Emmet. He used the American speeches to present himself in the position of Emmet. There was of course the site of his school (p. 67). Noting that Emmet undertook the complicated obligations attendant on forming a clandestine military organization, Pearse pointed out to his American audience the obvious parallel with himself: 'his task was just such a task as many of us have undertaken: he had to go through the same repellent routine of work, to deal with the hard, uncongenial details of correspondence and committee meetings; he had the same sordid difficulties that we have, yea, even the vulgar difficulty of want of funds' (p. 82).

By implication in both speeches, Pearse also accepted for himself the death Emmet died. 'There are in every generation those who shrink from the ultimate sacrifice, but there are in every generation those who make it with joy and laughter, and these are the salt of the generations, the heroes who stand midway between God and men' (pp. 65–6). Pearse intended the Americans to see him as one of those heroes. His style grows circumstantial and elaborate in presenting the account of Emmet's hanging and the mutilation of his body: 'his body was launched into the air. They say it swung for half-an-hour with terrible contortions before he died. When he was dead the comely head was severed from the body. A friend of mine knew an old woman who told him how the blood flowed down upon the pavement, and how she sickened with horror as she saw the dogs of the street lap up that noble blood' (pp. 70–1). He is similarly detailed in his account of Emmet's post-rebellion encounter with his house-keeper, Ann Devlin. When Emmet fled to his house in Rathfarnham, Ann at first rejected him for the supposed betrayal of escaping with his life. Pearse reported in both speeches that she greeted Emmet thus: ' "Musha, bad wel-come to you! Is Ireland lost by you, cowards that you are, to lead the people to destruction and then to leave them?" ' (pp. 68–9, p. 84). When Ann understood what had happened to Emmet, she repented her bitter words and tried to protect him. Pearse told his audience of her refusal to speak to the soldiers who questioned her about Emmet's hiding place and of her torture at their hands: 'They swung her up to a cart and half-hanged her several times; after each half-hanging she was revived and questioned: still the same answer. They pricked her breast with bayonets until the blood spurted out in their faces. They dragged her to prison and tortured her for days' (p. 84). Pearse's emphasis on Ann Devlin's role in Emmet's story is quite unusual. In the popular mythology of Emmet, the important woman is Sarah Curran, who was secretly engaged to him, whose vacillation about escaping with him to France led to his capture, and who is thought to have observed from a closed carriage as he was driven through the streets of Dublin to the execution site.[24] Pearse ignored the romantic possibilities in this situation to concen-trate on the servant girl to whom he assigned what were to him significant maternal qualities: she was the blood relation of men who fought in the Rising of 1798; she was nurturant and protective toward the patriot; she expected him to die for Ireland.

In the American speeches, Pearse unabashedly equated Emmet's death with Christ's: 'This man was faithful even unto the ignominy of the gallows, dying that his people might live, even as Christ died' (p. 71). In the final days of his life, Pearse lived out his identifications as patriot and redeemer; echoes of Emmet haunt those days. The Proclamation of the Republic, which he himself had drafted and which he read to mark the opening of the insurrection, was modelled on Emmet's proclamation in 1803.[25] In the early days of the Rising, Pearse was heard to remark that 'Emmet's two-hour revolt was already in the shade.'[26] In his speech to the British military court which tried him after the surrender, he presented himself simultaneously as leader of the Rising, doomed patriot, and divinely appointed sacrificial boy, roles which were summed up for him in the figure of Emmet.

I admit I was Commandant General, Commanding in Chief the forces of the Irish Republic which have been acting against you for the past week, and that I was President of their Provisional Government. I stand over all my acts and words done or spoken in those capacities. When I was a child of ten I went down on my bare knees by my bedside one night and promised God that I should devote my life to an effort to free my country. I have kept that promise.[27]

Pearse's statement to the military court, like Emmet's speech from the dock, defies England and unflinchingly accepts certain death. Its identification of himself in his thirty-seventh year at the climactic moment of his life with himself as a ten-year-old boy matches the statement in the autobiography that the achievements of his adult life were rooted in the childhood convalescence during which Aunt Margaret talked and sang to him of men who had died for Ireland. The innocent boy rebel is reciprocally linked for Pearse to the maternal figure who had placed on him the obligation of rebellion and death. Thus Ann Devlin is summoned into Pearse's version of the Emmet story. Thus Pearse facing his own execution is preoccupied with his relationship to his mother.

   In the remarkable documents written by him in the last three days of his life are two letters and two poems addressed to Mrs Pearse. In what was literally his last hour, Pearse completed one of the letters.[28] Pearse began the letter by expressing his regret that his mother was not allowed to visit him in the execution cell. He told her he had written a poem for her 'which would seem to be said by you about me' (p. 32). He assured her that he had been prepared for death by a priest and that he was serene. In the closing line, he presented to her and to his surviving family his death: 'I will call to you in my heart at the last moment' (p. 33). The execution-cell poem to which Pearse refers he entitled 'A Mother Speaks'.

> Dear Mary, that didst see they first-born Son
> Go forth to die amid the scorn of men
> For whom He died,
> Receive my first-born son into thy arms
> Who also hath gone out to die for men,
> And keep him by thee till I come to him.
> Dear Mary, I have shared thy sorrow,
> And soon shall share thy joy.[29]

This poem was of great importance to Pearse. Not only does he refer to it in the last letter, but he made two attempts to ensure that his mother would receive it after his death, leaving one copy with the officials at Arbour Hill Barracks and another with the priest who gave him the last rites at Kilmainham Jail. In the poem as in the letter, Pearse sees his mother acquiescing in his death, even as she mourns it.[30] His death is her sorrow and her glory. The moment of his death, when as the letter says, he will call to her in his heart, is the moment that justifies his life and transforms him into patriotic redeemer. The identifications of Robert Emmet with Christ and of himself with Emmet made in the American speeches have here become simplified; the dead body of Pearse is not his own, but Christ's. Written in emotional circumstances that can hardly be contemplated, this poem shows Pearse while still alive experiencing himself as non-existent. The poem expresses a double act of self-obliteration. With an arrogance which is the obverse of his abasement, he becomes the dead Christ. At the same time, he disappears into his mother; still alive, he speaks in her voice.

Pearse's death and the documents he left behind from the

days he lived through between the surrender on 29 April and the dawn of 3 May 1916 when he was shot, are matters both private and public, at the same time personal and deeply interwoven with the life of Irish society. In what turned out to be an accurate prediction, Pearse wrote his mother on 1 May, even before his court-martial and condemnation, of his certainty that the universally despised Rising would become valued in Ireland because of the execution sentences he expected for himself and the other leaders. Moreover, again accurately, he saw himself and her as public figures in the Ireland which would come to be after his death: 'People will say hard things of us now, but we shall be remembered by posterity and blessed by unborn generations. You too will be blessed because you were my mother.'[31]

At the end of 'A Mother Speaks', Pearse has become the figure of the dead Christ, indissolubly linked to the mourning mother within the single configuration of the pieta. The executed Pearse, now the statue-corpse of Christ, is clasped forever in the mother's stone embrace. Stephen Dedalus, forever poised for flight to Joyce's own exile, is the opposite of the bound and obliterated Pearse, but the opposed images of these two Irish sons have been generated by the same cultural experience. Joyce's commitment to exile and to art, which he saw as self-preserving, was the counterpart of Pearse's self-immolation in insurrectionary politics. Like Pearse's life-long progress toward a political execution, Joyce's exile was a matter both personal and deeply rooted in Irish social life. Joyce was a novelist of genius, and his separation from Ireland came to be understood in cosmopolitan modernist terms. But that wider understanding does not remove his exile and the work in which he enacted it from the context of that specific cultural experience, which as he remarked to Budgen in 1919, shaped him. The following examination of the themes of execution and of the fusion of mother and son in *Ulysses* is intended to suggest a way in which the novel may be related to that context. Although *Ulysses* is neither about the Rising and subsequent political processes in Ireland nor necessarily a conscious response to them, the novel and insurrectionary Irish politics ought to be set within the same cultural framework.

Robert Emmet first appears in *Ulysses* when Bloom at Paddy Dignam's funeral thinks of his secret burial at Glasnevin after he sees a rat crawl into a burial crypt.[32] Mr Kernan, passing Thomas Street, thinks of the legendary hanging: ' "Down there Emmet was hanged, drawn and quartered. Greasy black rope. Dogs licking the blood off the street" ' (p. 240). At the end of 'Sirens', Bloom trying to avoid the whore of the lane looks in the window of Lionel Marks's antique shop, sees Emmet's picture and thinks of Emmet's last words which, via a mistaken reference to Meyerbeer, he associates with Christ's. He deals with his flatulence, while in his mind reciting the famous conclusion of Emmet's speech from the dock. 'When my country takes her place among the nations of the earth, then and not till then, let my epitaph be written. I have done'.[33] Pearse called these words 'the most memorable ever uttered by an Irish man'.[34] Joyce's comic and degraded use of them immediately precedes the 'Cyclops' episode in which he presents the great parodic version of Emmet's execution. The brilliant comedy of Joyce's treatment of the execution scene resonates strangely with Pearse's enacting of the same scene in the only dream to which he would admit, and in his loving recreation of the death in the political speeches. For Pearse, the scene is always frozen. The innumerable spectators are motionless and silent; the Emmet figure, also motionless and silent, stands before them in boyish purity and nobility. The rigidity of the tableau is broken only by the violent contortions of the hanging man and by the flow of his blood in the dismemberment. Joyce's rendition of the execution scene is full of energy. Rain pours, lightning flashes. The assembled multitude, 'at the lowest computation five-hundred-thousand persons' (p. 306), brawls, admires the preparations for the sacrifice, and listens to a rendition of 'The Night Before Larry Was Stretched'. Joyce, unlike Pearse, uses the Sarah Curran element of the story when he presents the Emmet figure bidding farewell to his prospective bride on the gibbet

itself where she 'kissed passionately all the various suitable
areas of his person which the decencies of prison garb
permitted her ardour to reach' (p. 309). In *Ulysses*, the
patriot-victim is not executed; he disappears from the narrative as his fiancee becomes engaged to an Englishman, and
the new union is blessed by the military officer in charge of
the execution.

Joyce's presentation of the Irish patriotic execution in
'Cyclops' is a merciless commentary on the sentimentalizing
of horror in the service of nationalist propaganda, such
sentimentalizing as that practised by Pearse in his treatment
of the Emmet material. A falsification of the reality of human
suffering is involved in the discussion of the heroic erection
of the executed Invincible, Joe Brady. Hynes and Alf Bergan
perceive it as mysteriously connected to the martyr's poten-
cy: ' – Ruling passion strong in death, says Joe, as someone
said' (p. 304). Bloom, however, demystifies the erection;
thus he instructs his unappreciative companions in the phy-
siology of hanged men. The reality of the suffering of the
victim of an execution is expressed in the episode neither in
the Emmet parody nor in the citizen's catalogue of the dead
patriots, 'the invincibles and the old guard and the men of
sixtyseven and who fears to speak of ninetyeight and . . . all
the fellows that were hanged, drawn and transported for the
cause by drumhead courtmartial' (p. 305). It is to be found in
the narrator's account of the man lynched in Georgia: 'A lot
of Deadwood Dicks in slouch hats and they firing at a sambo
strung up on a tree with his tongue out and a bonfire under
him. Gob, they ought to drown him in the sea after and
electrocute and crucify him to make sure of their job' (p.
328).

The citizen, like Pearse, is on the side of the hanged rather
than the hangman. Yet it is the citizen whom Joyce casts as
Polyphemus, who murdered men by eating them. Though
the British Empire does the killing, Joyce identifies the
citizen's nationalist politics as incorporative and murderous.
Bloom tells the citizen that Irish nationalist force is the same
as the imperial force of England (p. 329), and presents his

own version of the nightmare of history as a futile cycle of coercion and resistance:

– But it's no use, says he. Force, hatred, history, all that. That's not life for men and women, insult and hatred. And everybody knows that it's the very opposite of that that is really life.
– What? says Alf.
– Love, says Bloom. I mean the opposite of hatred. (p. 333)

Bloom's answer is very appealing. It does not, however, resolve the issues raised by the citizen in his highly coloured but accurate survey of the exploitation of Ireland by England.[35] Bloom denounces the use of force, but he longs for social transformation so that the cycle of repression and hatred, which he himself has described, can be broken.

The attack on Bloom as a Jew leads him to assert his Irish nationality and to define the nation in terms which are the traditional terms of Irish nationalism: ' "A nation is the same people living in the same place" ' (p. 331). In spite of Ned Lambert's feeble joke, the concept that an Irishman is defined as a person who lives in Ireland is an enduring principle of Irish nationalism and certainly of Irish republicanism. Since the days of Wolfe Tone, Irish nationalists have opposed the attempt to exclude any section of the population of Ireland from membership in the nation which was to emerge from the revolutionary struggle. Pearse in his codification of a theory of Irish nationalism which appeared in a series of articles he published in the early months of 1916 expressed precisely Bloom's idea: 'Physically considered, what does a nation consist of? It consists of its men and women; all of its men and women, without any exceptions'.[36] Though John Wyse Nolan and Martin Cunningham agree that Bloom is the source of Arthur Griffith's Sinn Fein idea, Bloom himself makes only this blamelessly nationalist statement on Irish citizenship and his plea for a transformation of the processes of history. Bloom is an Irishman, but his Jewishness functions to protect him from participation in the mythology of insurrectionary nationalism. In this his Jewishness is like the exile of the Joycean novelist. The Jew and the artist are

Irishmen who yet resist assimilation into the processes of destruction by which Joyce, like Pearse, felt that Irish nationalism must realize itself. In so far as 'Cyclops' can be read as the expression of a political position, it rejects neither Irish nationalism nor the idea of a transformed politics for Ireland in which the cycle of force and hatred is broken. Joyce does however consider the warping and twisting of lives in the service of the insurrectionary idea. He is interested in the deformation of the self involved in submission to the assimilative–destructive processes of revolutionary nationalism; thus the technic of the chapter is gigantism, and the giant is a physical force nationalist who eats men. In 'Cyclops' Joyce chose to consider the inhuman deformation of Irish revolutionaries without directly engaging the Rising. In fact, the parodic passages in the episode and the use of the nameless narrator as well as the 1904 time setting may be thought of as strategies to express Joyce's distance from the political content of the episode. In this sense, the complicated narrative devices of 'Cyclops' are the antithesis of the terrifying simplicity of Pearse's poem to his mother from the execution cell.

The themes of radical social change, execution, and the fusion of mother and son coalesce in 'Circe'. Joyce first works out this complex of themes in the episode in relation to Bloom. Bloom's fantasy of a transformed society begins with his wish for personal power rather than his concern with the Irish historical situation. Bloom sees himself as Lord Mayor of Dublin .(p. 478); he quickly becomes the ' "undoubted emperor president and king chairman, the most serene and potent and very puissant ruler of this realm" ' (p. 482). He commands construction of the city of the new society, ' "the new Bloomusalem in the Nova Hibernia of the future!" ' (p. 484). The building of the new city in the shape of the pork kidney he has eaten for breakfast involves a grotesque version of revolution in that it brings social disruption and death: '*Government offices are temporarily transferred to railway sheds. Numerous houses are razed to the ground. The inhabitants are lodged in barrels and boxes. . . . Several paupers fall from a ladder. A part of the walls of Dublin, crowded with loyal sightseers, collapses*' (pp. 484–5). Bloom administers justice and advice, but his reign ends; he is accused of Parnell's crime, and the mob demands that he, like the Negro in Georgia, be lynched and burned (p. 493). The call for his execution is immediately followed by Bloom's transformation into a woman, then into a mother in labour in the act of delivering 'eight male yellow and white children' (p. 494). Bloom is then announced as the Messiah (p. 497), condemned by the inquisition, and executed by burning; he achieves apotheosis in the litany recited by the daughters of Erin (p. 498). This bizarre fantasy duplicates Pearse's vision of patriotic insurrection and personal obliteration. Thus even though Bloom sees his politics as enlightened, humane, and non-violent, his fantasy demands that the transformation of society which he brings about be linked to his execution. Moreover, the execution is associated with a fantasy of the fusion of mother and son as Bloom's body becomes a woman's body in the moment of giving birth to the eight metallic sons within it.

These same elements are presented in the final sections of 'Circe' in relation to Stephen Dedalus and his fantasy of confrontation with his dead mother. When Mrs Dedalus appears, she is associated with Emmet by means of the carrion-eating rat Bloom had earlier seen at Glasnevin. She is both eaten by the grave, *'her face worn and noseless'* (p. 579), and ravenous herself to eat. To her son, she is lemur, ghoul, hyena, and most horribly ' "The corpsechewer! Raw head and bloody bones!" ' (p. 581). These epithets cast the penitential submission which Stephen sees her asking of him as his assimilation by her and thus his destruction within her. This disappearance of the son as he is fused with the mother is expressed in the moment before Stephen breaks the lamp when Mrs Dedalus speaks *'in the agony of her deathrattle'* (p. 582), claiming for herself the role of suffering and redemptive Christ: ' "Have mercy on Stephen, Lord, for my sake! Inexpressible was my anguish when expiring with love, grief and agony on Mount Calvary" ' (p. 582). This fusion of mother and son in one figure as the dying Christ conveys exactly what Pearse conveys in the pietà figure in the poem to his mother. In the fantasy of Stephen, when she becomes Christ, Mrs Dedalus obliterates her son just as in the fantasy of Pearse, he is merged with his mother as she arranges his body for the eternal embrace of the pietà. Bloom's transformation into a woman bearing sons is the grotesque variation on this fused figure of mother and son. Joyce presents the breaking of the lamp with words Stephen has previously associated with war (p. 24) and with the Clerkenwell Prison explosion (p. 43): '*Time's livid final flame leaps and, in the following darkness, ruin of all space, shattered glass and toppling masonry*' (p. 583). Each time these words are used in *Ulysses*, they present a violent attack on boundaries: the walls of the city, the walls of the prison, and in 'Circe' on the most primitive of all boundaries, the line which separates mother from child and therefore self from world. In the assault on boundaries, organized space breaks down into chaos. This is the exploded moment, the undifferentiated space in which Pearse disappeared. Stephen Dedalus, raising Siegfried's dragon-slaying sword, refuses to be destroyed in it, and his mother disappears. The breaking of the lamp is his retaliatory and successful assault on mother/Ireland/church which, like Pearse, he saw as requiring of him his obliteration.

The events that follow the breaking of the lamp reinforce the connection between political revolution and the bond between mother and son. Stephen flees the brothel and becomes involved in the encounter with the Irish prostitutes and the English soldiers. He tells Private Carr that he is striving to kill priest and king in his own mind (p. 589), thus stressing that the liberation for which he searches is his own, not his country's. As the conflict between him and Carr develops, Stephen reinforces this point: ' "But I say: Let my country die for me. Up to the present it has done so" ' (p. 591). The ancient sufferings of mother and Ireland demand that son and citizen accept for himself the maternal and national pain. Stephen has refused to made this acceptance, thus in his mind condemning the country to a destruction which he nevertheless does not want for it: ' "I don't want it to die. Damn death. Long live life!" ' (p. 591). The execution theme enters Stephen's fantasy through the reappearance of elements from 'Cyclops'. The citizen calls for vengeance against the English for their hanging of Irish patriots (p. 593). Rumbold appears and hangs not Robert Emmet but the innocent and betrayed croppy boy, whose last words are a strangled admission of his guilt at not praying for his dead mother (p. 594). The boy dies with a gigantic erection; his sperm falls on the ground like Emmet's blood.

As Private Carr grows more outraged, old Gummy Granny appears to Stephen and is greeted with the formula of his hatred and fear of Ireland: ' "The old sow that eats her farrow!" ' (p. 595). At the climax of Stephen's argument with the soldiers, the cry ' "Dublin's burning! Dublin's burning! On fire, on fire!" ' releases a series of terrifying images (pp. 598–9). It is through them, I suggest, that the allegedly stagnant Dublin of the novel's 1904 is penetrated by the burning and revolutionary Dublin of 1916 and afterwards. Dublin becomes a military battleground; the carnage of war gives way to a condition of total boundary collapse; no line separates day and night, living and dead, characters of history and characters of fiction, rebels and members of parliament. The Black Mass is celebrated on the naked body of Mina Purefoy, nine months pregnant after her three-day labour, once again fused with the body of her son. At the consecration of the Mass, Gummy Granny presses the dagger into Stephen's hand, urging him to murder Carr, begin the revolution, and surrender himself to his own execution: ' "Remove him acushla. At 8 : 35 a.m. you will be in heaven and Ireland will be free!" ' (p. 600). Instead, Stephen is assaulted and knocked out. The chaos of transformations gives way to the order of paternal relationship; Bloom the father rescues and protects Stephen the son.

Pearse and Joyce both thought that Ireland, by the necessities of its past had to take its freedom in the sacrificial blood of Irishmen. For both of them, to think about the process by which Ireland would be separated from England was to think about personal obliteration, which each saw as a merging of himself with the mother. Pearse gave himself to that moment of fusion and personal annihilation; Joyce withheld himself from it. But Joyce's refusal comes out of the same culture that produced Pearse's acceptance. Joyce understood the act of self-assertion which constituted his work as an artist in relation to what he thought was Ireland's call for his self-immolation. The significant presence in *Ulysses* of the same concepts and images used by Pearse to articulate his patriot-martyr's response to Ireland indicates, I suggest, a deep relationship between Joyce's novel, the way Pearse died in 1916, and the way in which Ireland in the years immediately following his death came to interpret it.

1. Valery Larbaud, 'A propos de James Joyce et d'*Ulysse*', *Nouvelle revue francaise*, 24, January 1925, pp. 5–17. Reprinted in Valery Larbaud, *Oeuvres completes* (Paris, 1951), vol. 3, pp. 401–16. See Richard Ellmann, *The Consciousness of Joyce* (New York, 1977), p. 141.
2. See the editor's introduction to *Memoirs of Desmond Fitzgerald 1913–1916* (London, 1968), p. xi.
3. See Joyce's letter of 20 March 1922, to Stanislaus Joyce in Richard Ellmann, ed., *Letters of James Joyce* (New York, 1966), vol. 3, p. 61.
4. Desmond Ryan, *Remembering Sion* (London, 1934), p. 43.
5. Frank Budgen, *James Joyce and the Making of Ulysses* (Bloomington, 1960), p. 152.
6. James Joyce, *A Portrait of the Artist as a Young Man*, ed. Chester G. Anderson (New York, 1968), p. 203.
7. See F. X. Martin, '1916 – Myth, Fact, and Mystery', *Studia Hibernica*, no. 7, 1967, pp. 19–21, p. 39, and F. X. Martin, 'The 1916 Rising – a *Coup d'Etat* or a "Bloody Protest"?', *Studia Hibernica*, no. 8, 1968, p. 133. See also Ruth Dudley Edwards, *Patrick Pearse: The Triumph of Failure* (London, 1977), pp. 323–44.
8. Martin, '1916 – Myth, Fact, and Mystery', pp. 19–21.
9. Richard Ellmann, *James Joyce* (New York, 1959 and London, 1966), p. 62.
10. See the references to Hughes in James Joyce, *Stephen Hero* (New York, 1963), pp. 59–60, pp. 82–3, p. 103. Like Hughes,

Pearse was in the time period covered in *Stephen Hero* active in the Gaelic League, a fledgling orator, and a law student at the King's Inns. Stanislaus Joyce in *My Brother's Keeper* (New York, 1969), p. 165, points out that Hughes's poem was actually written by Louis Walsh, who like Hughes was an Ulsterman and who also studied law.

11. *Three Lectures on Gaelic Topics* was published in March 1898 (Edwards, *Patrick Pearse*, p. 23). It was reprinted in *Collected Works of Padraic H. Pearse* (Dublin, 1924). This collection of Pearse's work was edited by Desmond Ryan, though Ryan's name appears as editor only of one of the five volumes in the edition. Edwards notes that this edition, of which there have been numerous reissues, was not dated originally but appeared in Dublin between 1917 and 1922 (p. 362). The volumes were not numbered. *Three Lectures on Gaelic Topics* is to be found in the volume entitled *Songs of the Irish Rebels and Specimens from an Irish Anthology; Some Aspects of Irish Literature; Three Lectures on Gaelic Topics.*

12. Reprinted in *The Critical Writings of James Joyce*, ed. Ellsworth Mason and Richard Ellmann (New York, 1964), pp. 69–72.

13. Pearse, 'Some Aspects of Irish Literature', in *Songs of the Irish Rebels* etc., p. 155.

14. Joyce, *A Portrait*, p. 181.

15. In 'The Folk Songs of Ireland' from *Three Lectures on Gaelic Topics* (*Songs of the Irish Rebels* etc., pp. 197–215), Pearse develops the idea of the power and beauty of the folk imagination in Ireland and its exalted morality.

16. James Joyce, 'The Soul of Ireland', in *Critical Writings*, p. 103.

17. Padraic Pearse, *Plays, Stories, Poems* (Dublin, 1917), p. 333.

18. See the two articles by Martin previously cited and Francis Shaw, 'The Canon of Irish History – A Challenge', *Studies*, vol. 61, no. 242, Summer 1972, pp. 115–53.

19. Pearse's autobiographical work was published in *The Home Life of Padraig Pearse*, ed. Mary Brigid Pearse (Dublin, 1934), pp. 13–40. M. B. Pearse gives no indication of the period in which Pearse wrote the autobiographical fragment. I am suggesting the 1914 to 1916 period because of Pearse's references to his role in military planning and national policy. Pearse was sworn into the Irish Republican Brotherhood in late 1913; in September, 1915, he was elected to the Supreme Council of the Irish Republican Brotherhood and placed on its Military Council. See Edwards, *Patrick Pearse*, p. 180, pp. 241–2.

20. For a consideration of messianism in Irish political life, see William Thompson's *The Imagination of an Insurrection* (New

York, 1967). For a consideration of messianism in Irish cultural life, see Herbert Howarth, *The Irish Writers: Literature and Nationalism 1880–1940* (New York, 1959). For a survey of messianic beliefs in Irish history, see Patrick O'Farrell, 'Millenialism, Messianism and Utopianism in Irish History', *Anglo-Irish Studies*, vol. 2, 1976, pp. 45–68. The best critique of Pearse's messianism is Shaw's article previously cited.

21. Pearse, *Plays, Stories, Poems*, pp. 45–67.
22. Padraic Pearse, *The Story of a Success*, ed. Desmond Ryan (Dublin, 1917), p. 7. This history of St Enda's was compiled from Pearse's column in the school's periodical, *An Macaomh*. All references to St Enda's are from this volume of *Collected Works*.
23. Padraic Pearse, *Political Speeches and Writings*, pp. 64–75, pp. 76–87. This volume appears as part of *Collected Works*. All references to these speeches are from this volume.
24. In the Christmas 1910, issue of *An Macaomh*, Pearse wrote of reading Stephen Gwynn's *Robert Emmet*. Gwynn's book concentrates on Emmet's relation to Sarah Curran.
25. Edwards, *Patrick Pearse*, p. 280.
26. Desmond Ryan, *The Rising* (Dublin, 1949), p. 143.
27. Piaras F. Mac Lochlainn, *Last Words: Letters and Statements of the Leaders Executed after the Rising at Easter 1916* (Dublin, 1971), p. 28.
28. Mac Lochlainn, *Last Words*, holds that the letter was completed within an hour of Pearse's execution (p. 34). The quotations from Pearse's letter are taken from Mac Lochlainn's book.
29. Mac Lochlainn, *Last Words*, p. 22.
30. In another poem written in Arbour Hill Barracks on 1 May, 'To My Mother' (Mac Lochlainn, *Last Days*, p. 21), Pearse presents his death as a gift to his mother.
31. Mac Lochlainn, *Last Days*, p. 19. Note that this letter, like the 1915 poem previously cited, uses the resonance to the Magnificat to associate the pregnancy of Mary/Mrs Pearse with Pearse's execution.
32. James Joyce, *Ulysses* (New York, 1961), p. 114.
33. *Ulysses*, p. 291. For a complete text of Emmet's speech, see T. M. Kettle, ed., *Irish Orators and Oratory* (Dublin, n.d.), pp. 322–32.
34. Pearse, *Political Speeches*, p. 70.
35. Joyce himself praises Ireland's ancient culture and makes many of the citizen's charges against England in 'Ireland, Island of Saints and Sages' (*Critical Writing*, pp. 156–72).
36. Pearse, 'The Sovereign People', *Political Speeches*, p. 338. The point is also made in the Proclamation of the Irish Republic.

Some structuring devices in Joyce's 'The Dead'

HUBERT McDERMOTT

'The Dead' is not simply 'a linchpin in Joyce's work',[1] as Richard Ellman argues: it is also one of the great short stories of modern times. The skill and ingenuity which Joyce displays in structuring the story contributes significantly to its success. This is not to say that the structure of 'The Dead' is unduly prominent: on the contrary, only several close readings of the text will reveal the subtlety and complexity of the structure. There is, therefore, a major 'detective story' element in 'The Dead'. While a reader invariably derives benefit from a second reading of any play, poem, or story, two or more readings are almost a *sine qua non* for a true appreciation of 'The Dead'.

The most obvious structuring device is contained in the title itself. At first it seems to refer simply to Michael Furey who is as surely the mainspring of this story as the Ghost is in *Hamlet*. Later, we realize that although Michael Furey is dead, and has been for some time, he lives on, a vital force, in the memory of Gretta Conroy. Soon, the 'living' are revealed to be 'dead', to have, in one of the phrases of the story, 'perished alive'.[2] The greater part of the story is taken up with a party, normally the epitome of liveliness, but there appear to be only two people present who are alive. Miss Ivors is one of these, and she leaves early, as if to emphasize that she is not one of the dead: Freddy Malins, too, appears to be alive, but he has simply escaped from the dead for a few hours through inebriation. The New Year's Eve party is being given by two old spinsters and their niece, Mary Jane. The two old women – the Misses Morkan – have not very long to live, and the relatively young Mary Jane, like Maria, in 'Clay' appears to have little to look forward to in life. Even

her party-piece is admired only for the professional manner
of its execution.

The choice of the name Conroy for the protagonist of 'The
Dead', is an interesting one. 'Conroy' is one of the usual
anglicizations of the Irish surname, O'Conaire. It is the
maidservant Lily who first directs our attention to the Irish
form of the name. When Lily pronounces 'Conroy' with
three syllables, she is, unwittingly, we presume, close to the
pronunciation of the name in its original, Irish, form. It is
appropriate that Gabriel should smile 'at the three syllables
she had given his surname' (p. 175), in view of his attitude
towards Irish. Of greater interest is the similarity in
pronunciation – in the Irish dialect of the West of Ireland, at
any rate – between the Irish words *conaire*, a keeper of
hounds, and *cónra*, a coffin. 'Conroy' could, therefore, be
regarded as a Joycean anglicization of *cónra*. That Gabriel
Conroy could be renamed Gabriel Coffin is particularly
appropriate in the context of the story as a whole, and
specifically in the light of the important dinner-table conversation which turns to talk of coffins.

The dead as a structuring device reappears in other,
various, guises during the course of the story. A good
example is Joyce's use of pictures – those of Romeo and
Juliet, the two murdered princes, and an imagined painting
entitled *Distant Music*. Romeo and Juliet are associated with
death as well as with love; the link between the murdered
princes and death is self-evident; and the imagined painting,
Distant Music is essentially concerned – though unknown to
either Gabriel or the reader at that point – with a dead man,
Michael Furey.

The picture of Romeo and Juliet is also important for the
more conventional association of these two characters with a
rich, sensual, love. In 'The Dead' Michael Furey is Romeo,
Gretta Conroy, Juliet. Michael Furey commits a version of
suicide by going to see Gretta on the night before she left
Galway. 'I think he died for me' (p. 217), Gretta tells Gabriel.
Gretta, however, is a significant variation on Juliet. Having
lost her Romeo she too commits 'suicide' – though not for

Michael Furey – by marrying a dead Dubliner, Gabriel Con-roy. Gabriel and Dublin assist in the killing of the vital West-of-Ireland personality of Gretta, and she becomes, eventually, just another dead Dubliner. But never fully so: the living memory of Michael Furey and his love for her is her saving grace. It will be the salvation of Gabriel too, eventually. Gretta refuses to allow the memory of Michael Furey to die and thus remains faithful to her Romeo after a fashion.

Joyce has aimed at further effects based on the Romeo and Juliet painting, and these too play a part in structuring the story. The scene from *Romeo and Juliet* which is portrayed in the living-room picture is, we are informed, the balcony scene. Joyce creates two, perhaps even three balcony scenes in 'The Dead', effecting significant variations on the original, Shakespearean, one. The first balcony scene coincides with what is the turning point of the story, i.e., Gretta's listening to Bartell D'arcy singing 'The Lass of Aughrim'. Joyce describes the scene as follows:

Gabriel had not gone to the door with the others. He was in a dark part of the hall gazing up the staircase. A woman was standing near the top of the first flight, in the shadow also. He could not see her face but he could see the terra-cotta and salmon-pink panels of her skirt which the shadow made appear black and white. It was his wife. She was leaning on the banisters, listening to something. Gabriel was surprised at her stillness and strained his ear to listen also . . . There was grace and mystery in her attitude as if she were a symbol of something. He asked himself what is a woman standing on the stairs in the shadow, listening to distant music, a symbol of. If he were a painter he would paint her in that attitude. Her blue felt hat would show off the bronze of her hair against the darkness, and the dark panels of her skirt would show off the light ones. *Distant Music* he would call the picture if he were a painter (pp. 206–7).

In this balcony scene Gabriel and Gretta are affected consider-ably, each in a quite distinct and different way. The reawakened memory of her lover, Michael Furey, affects Gretta not just mentally, but physically as well. It is the

'grace and mystery in her attitude' which arouses Gabriel
sexually. When Gretta eventually comes down to the hallway
Gabriel notices that she is in the 'same attitude as she had
been on the stairs and seemed unaware of the talk about her.
At last she turned towards them and Gabriel saw that there
was colour on her cheeks and that her eyes were shining. *A
sudden tide of joy went leaping out of his heart*' (p. 209; my
italics). The memory of Michael Furey affects Gretta in such
a way as to arouse her husband, but this same memory
makes Gretta totally blind to the lust, desire, and intentions
of her husband.

The scene which 'The Lass of Aughrim' recreates in the
mind of Gretta Conroy is a 'balcony' one which had occurred
many years previously in Galway. In this scene, Gretta is
upstairs in her grandmother's house in Nun's Island, pack-
ing, getting ready to leave for Dublin the following day,
when she hears gravel being thrown against her window. It is
her 'Romeo', Michael Furey, who has thrown the gravel in
order to attract her attention; and when Gretta runs down-
stairs to him, she find him 'shivering, at the end of the wall
where there was a tree' (p. 218).

As one reads 'The Dead' it is apparent that, as Gretta
Conroy stands on a staircase in the house of the Misses
Morkan, not far from a picture of the balcony scene in *Romeo
and Juliet*, she is, in conjunction with her husband, creating a
new balcony scene. The full extent of Joyce's achievement in
this balcony scene only becomes apparent, however, towards
the end of the story. Only then is it clear that, as Gretta and
Gabriel are involved in their balcony scene on Usher's Island,
Gretta has been preoccupied with the memory of another,
momentous, balcony scene – the one in which she and
Michael Furey had taken part many years previously. The
significant effect of the counterpointing of the Usher's Island
and the Nun's Island balcony scenes needs no elaboration.

'The Dead' ends with yet another balcony scene. On this
occasion, Gabriel Conroy is lying on his bed in the Gresham
Hotel, when 'a few light taps on the pane made him turn to
the window' (p. 219). These 'few light taps' immediately call

to mind the gravel thrown against the window pane in Nun's Island. It is as if Michael Furey is trying to attract the attention of Gabriel Conroy on this occasion. If this is his aim, he certainly succeeds, for Gabriel's thoughts immediately turn to Michael Furey, lying in a lonely churchyard on a hill. Michael and Gabriel have, between them, created the final balcony scene of the story and thereby strengthened a relationship between them which had come into being a short time previously.

Distant Music is the other picture which plays a part in the structuring of Joyce's story, and it is associated with both death and music. Gabriel Conroy is so captivated by the grace and mystery of his wife's attitude as she stands on the staircase at the end of the party that, 'if he were a painter he would paint her in that attitude. *Distant Music* he would call the painting if he were a painter' (p. 207). Joyce has surrounded this title with several, subtle, ironies. By 'distant' music, Gabriel means simply to convey the effect on his wife of music coming from a room some distance from where his wife is standing. But the music which Gretta hears is distant in a quite different way: she hears again 'The Lass of Aughrim' as it was sung to her many years previously by Michael Furey. Later, Gabriel hears distant music also:

In one letter that he had written to her [Gretta] he had said: Why is it that words like these seem to me dull and cold? Is it because there are no words tender enough to be your name? Like distant music these words that he had written years before were borne towards him from the past (p. 211).

At this point in 'The Dead', 'distant' has come to mean the distance of years for Gabriel also. But the gulf between him and his wife, emphasized throughout the story, remains as wide as ever: the music he now hears is that of his own words while the music Gretta heard was that of another.

If the final story of *Dubliners* were to have a title other than 'The Dead' it would obviously have to be one in which music would feature, since music is only second to the dead in its prominence in the story. The occasion of the story is a

musical one, the annual dance of the Misses Morkan. Kate
and Mary Jane teach music, and Julia is leading soprano in
Adam and Eve's church. In addition, Mary Jane 'has the
organ in Haddington Road' (p. 173). As well as friends and
relations, the members of Julia's choir, Kate's and Mary
Jane's pupils 'that were grown up enough', were invited to
the party. During the course of the night, Mary Jane plays
her party-piece on the piano, and Aunt Julia sings 'Arrayed
for the Bridal'. The singing of another song, 'The Lass of
Aughrim', plays a major role in the story, and marks its
turning point. It reminds Gretta of a life and a love she once
knew, and the memory, once rekindled, does not simply die
as quickly as it appeared: it goes on to haunt her for the
remainder of her waking hours on that night. Gabriel is
totally unaware of of his wife's true feelings, and this leads
him, unsuspecting, to a shattering rebuff, followed by an
epiphany. We discover later in the story that Michael Furey
often sang for Gretta, and that he 'was going to study singing
only for his health' (p. 217). It is in the context of this remark
of Gretta's that the subsequent conversation at the supper-
table and Gabriel's after-dinner speech, become such an
organic part of the structure of the story. Conversation at the
Misses Morkans' supper table commences with a discussion
of the opera company then playing at the Theatre Royal, and
soon turns to a consideration of the great singers of the past.
The particular relevance of this conversation to the story in
general is perhaps best highlighted by Aunt Kate, who
remarks: 'For me . . . there was only one tenor. To please
me, I mean. But I suppose none of you ever heard of him
(p. 197). Once again, it is only a second reading of the
story which reveals the full significance of this remark. For
Gretta, too, there has been, and still is, 'only one tenor',
Michael Furey: and obviously none of the partygoers ever
heard of him either.

A second reading of 'The Dead' also reveals the ironies in
Gabriel's speech at the end of the meal. He intends to use in
his speech the sentence: 'One feels that one is listening to a
thought-tormented music' (p. 189). This ironic remark is

complemented in the speech itself when Gabriel says: 'But we are living in . . . a thought-tormented world' (p. 200–1). Some of the remainder of Gabriel's speech is worth quoting, to show how the ghostly presence of Michael Furey lurks continually behind the words:

Listening tonight to the names of all those great singers of the past it seemed to me, I must confess, that we were living in a less spacious age: and if they are beyond recall, let us hope, at least, that in gatherings such as this we shall still speak of them with pride and affection, still cherish in our hearts the memory of those dead and gone great ones whose fame the world will not willingly let die . . . But yet . . . there are always in gatherings such as this sadder thoughts that will recur to our minds: thoughts of the past, of youth, of changes, of absent faces that we miss here tonight (p. 201).

Joyce manages to create many associations between music and death in 'The Dead'. The most obvious of these are in the supper-table conversation and in Gabriel's speech. The story of the ballad 'The Lass of Aughrim', the picture *Distant Music*, the ironic 'Arrayed for the Bridal', and Michael Furey himself, all emphasize this connection.

Weather conditions – in particular, rain, snow, and cold – are also used by Joyce as a means of structuring his story. The role of snow has been investigated and analysed by many critics, yet it still remains something of a mystery. At the start of 'The Dead', the differing attitudes of Gabriel and Gretta towards the snow accentuates the difference in their personalities. The story ends with a reference to snow, too, when Gabriel, for the first time, comes close to a true understanding of his wife. As a result of the events on this New Year's Eve, a new and vital relationship will be formed between Gretta and Gabriel. But this is not the only relationship which the night will have formed: a new variation on the eternal triangle will have come into being. For the two 'living-dead' men in the story, Michael and Gabriel, will also have had a bond forged between them. The forging of this new bond recalls, in part, at least, the bond between Gretta and Michael. The resemblance between the scene in Nun's

Island and the one in the Gresham Hotel has already been noted. But the resemblance does not end there. When Gabriel, in the hotel, has his attention drawn to the snow by the tapping of snowflakes on the window, he begins to trace the path of the snow right across Ireland:

Yes the newspapers were right: snow was general all over Ireland. It was falling on every part of the dark central plain, on the treeless hills, falling softly upon the Bog of Allen and, farther westward, softly falling into the dark mutinous Shannon waves. It was falling, too, upon every part of the lonely churchyard on the hill where Michael Furey lay buried (p. 220).

The snow, then, is used to create a very effective link between Gabriel and Michael.

At the start of 'The Dead' there is continual emphasis on the coldness of the night, a coldness associated with the snow. When Kate and Julia Morkan presume that Gretta must be 'perished alive' the metaphorical implications of the remark are evident. Michael Furey, on the other hand, had been literally perished alive on the eventful night in Galway. Gretta describes him as 'shivering', and tells him he will 'get his death in the rain'. Michael Furey, in fact, dies within a week.

One final, minor, though nonetheless ingenious, structuring device in 'The Dead', is Joyce's use of the two islands – Usher's Island and Nun's Island. The contemporary events of 'The Dead' are set mainly in the Misses Morkans' house in Usher's Island in Dublin. It is while she is on this island that Gretta Conroy is made to recollect an event on another island many years previously.

1. Richard Ellman, *James Joyce* (New York, 1959 and London, 1966), p. 261.
2. James Joyce, *Dubliners* (London, Penguin Books, 1956), p. 175. All subsequent page references are to this edition.

Sound and sense in Samuel Beckett's drama and fiction

JOHN P. DE SOLLAR

L'homme parle seulement pour autant qu'il repond au langage en écoutant ce qu'il lui dit. Heidegger.

L'être humain est une créature chantante qui unit la musique à la pensée. W. von Humboldt.[1]

In hearing Beckett's work we find it. Therefore we can only properly understand his meaning and intent by opening our senses to the myriad patterns of sound and silence in his fiction and plays.[2] Indeed Beckett has described his prose as 'a matter of fundamental sounds . . . made as fully as possible'[3], and nowhere is this aural interplay more apparent, or more strikingly conveyed, than in a recorded reading given by Jack MacGowran under Beckett's close supervision.[4] This chapter will examine, in chronological order, selected passages in the record from *Malone Dies, The Unnamable* and *Endgame* in an attempt to see why and how his prose increases in its eloquence and depth of expression as the verbal means are systematically reduced.

In his search for a *cleaner* form of prose, one unmuddied by convention and no longer 'abstracted to death',[5] Beckett has created something that is 'not only to be read. It is to be looked at and listened to'.[6] In other words he has narrowed the gap between language and reality, inasmuch as simplicity of style allows a greater freedom of reaction. The lack of specificity also expands the desperate truth of some statements while paradoxically highlighting the deep obscurity of others. As he once admitted to a friend:

I am interested in the shape of ideas. There is a wonderful sentence in Augustine: 'Do not despair; one of the thieves was saved. Do not presume; one of the thieves was damned'. That sentence has a wonderful shape. It is the shape that matters.[7]

This *shape* is intimately related to the tone and feel of his prose: his wonderful rhythms, the way he weighs his words, the authority he gives to each and the silences between them. There are similar patterns in the universal language of music, yet it is more directly visceral in effect and remains essentially an ineffable experience. Nonetheless, what Boehme has called the ideal language, *die sensualische Sprache*,[8] inheres in the form and movement of Beckett's prose. He reveals his commitment in an interview with Gabriel d'Aubarède: 'J'ai conçu *Molloy* et la suite le jour où j'ai pris conscience de ma bêtise. Alors, je me suis mis à écrire les choses que je sens.'[9] What he feels is conveyed with a unique, reverberating depth and intensity in the MacGowran reading, where words sometimes step beyond language in an attempt 'de restituer par voie d'operations conscientes la valeur de sensualité et la puissance émotive des choses'.[10]

Beckett's creative solipsism, moreover, enables him to discover within himself the ability to captivate our deepest feelings, since he believes that 'the only possible spiritual development is in the sense of depth' and consequently:

> The only fertile research is excavatory, immersive, a contraction of the spirit, a descent. The artist is active, but negatively, shrinking from the nullity of extracircumferential phenomena, drawn in to the core of the eddy.[11]

This attitude is by no means original to Beckett, nor is his observation on Jack Yeats's art, 'L'artiste qui joue son être est de nulle part. Et il n'a pas de frères',[12] since all true artists are solitary explorers of interior space. But few of them maintain such a profound and ruthless progression towards realizing these principles in their work. Hugh Kenner remarks upon a similar sense of timelessness when he describes Beckett's prose style:

> He is the principal master in our time of the formal declarative sentence . . . Every such sentence advances the narrative, or the argument, to an exact and measurable degree; there is no ellipsis, no *rubato*, no homely leap of the precipitate heart. The *pace* of his prose is even and indomitable, utterly unrelated to the pace of events.[13]

Kenner's description could easily be applied to the opening
section of *Malone Dies*:

I shall soon be quite dead at last | in spite of all. Perhaps | next
month. Then it will be the month of April | or of | May. For
the year is still young, a thousand little signs tell me so. Perhaps I
am wrong, perhaps I shall survive Saint John the Baptist's
Day | and even the Fourteenth of July, festival of | freedom.
Indeed I would not put it past me to pant on to the Transfiguration,
not to speak of the Assumption. But I do not think so, I do not
think I am wrong in saying that these | rejoicings | will take place
in my absence, this year . . . I could die to-day if I wished, merely
by making a little effort. But it is just as well to let myself die,
quietly, without rushing things . . . I shall be | neutral, and inert.
No difficulty there . . . Yes | I shall be natural | at last, I shall suffer
more, then less, without drawing any conclusions, I shall pay | less
heed to myself, I shall be neither hot | nor cold | any more, I
shall be | tepid, I shall die | tepid, without enthusiasm . . . I am
content, necessarily, but not to the point of clapping my hands . . .
I am satisfied, there, I have enough, I am repaid, I need nothing
more. Let me say before I go any further | that I forgive | nobody.
I wish them all | an atrocious life | and then the fires | and ice | of
hell | and in the "execrable generations to come | an honoured |
name.[14]

The same quiet control is evident in the introductory sentences, with their compressed display of apparent apathy.
But the sombre economy of means only amplifies the
self-conscious undervoice of the creator mocking his creation. Moreover, this whisper grows imperceptively louder as
the monologue progresses, and results in a gradual transformation from subdued irony to a form of sophisticated
levity riotously out of key with its subject, though always
more muffled and implied than similar passages from *Watt*.
The numerous pauses and hesitations in the reading simultaneously enhance this irony and act as a caveat to the
complacent, careless reader, asking him to acknowledge the
delicate union of sound and sense. For instance, small
nuances such as the lengthy pause after 'inert', immediately
remind us that in Beckett's world 'It makes no difference
how one waits or what one does while waiting; only the
necessity of waiting has any significance.'[15] Or consider in

the following line, 'Yès | I shall be nàtural | at làst, . . . I shall die | tèpid, without enthusiasm.' It is a beautifully constructed sentence, without a single trace of imprecision and the relentless *pace* that Kenner speaks of is illustrated in the repeated 'shall'. Its insistent semantic propulsion to an anticipated future, also conveys by systematic repetition a concomitant sense of circularity and stasis.

However the comic undercurrents and breezy air of imperturbability do not last for long, because Beckett has a sceptic's habit of giving due weight to every side of a question. Consequently, Malone's passionless proclamation, 'I am content, nècessarily, . . . I need nòthing mòre', should arouse our suspicions. Obviously the professed tone of apathy is too lacquered with seeming indifference to be wholly authentic, and it remains for the veiled, though violent sibilance and assonance in the final two sentences to vitiate his claims for self-determination. But it is only in the last sentence that Malone's smouldering emotions are fully vented. There he erupts with a snarling savagery that reaches its culmination in the verbal flaying of 'nȁme', thus making manifest a valiant assertion of the 'I' of self-identity. Yet the brutality and venom of that final curse is not cathartic, despite its energy. It is only sadly ironic in the way it exposes the vacuity of a life without hope of redemption.

The recording in short, gives a superb rendering of Malone's inevitable and painful transition to vicious misanthropy, whereas in a simple *reading* of the text we might easily overlook the overt turbulence of 'nȁme' or the rasping severity of adjectives like 'atrȍcious' and 'ȅxecrable'. Hence by hearing the words delivered in a manner intended by the writer, we enter into a microcosm of immensely powerful feelings that reverberate in the memory, so that Malone's gesturings are, in the end, instructive rather than destructive or demeaning. They unsettle the shroud that habit weaves about our daily lives and transmit a sensation of sardonic ebullience vying with conformity and spiritual restraints, despite a horribly reduced physical and material universe.

The frantic, breathless, almost subterranean mania of the

final speech in *The Unnamable* presents however, a consciousness bereft even of Cartesian doubts, which has advanced to a
state where dualism is (fundamentally) no longer a question.
But while this oft-quoted passage represents an extreme and
almost desperate reaction to the inherent limits of language,
it is never despairing. That would infer a judgement or
valuation, both of which Beckett avoids assiduously and
without false modesty. Instead his only concern, as one
highly self-conscious about his task as a writer, is how to
transmute language so as to give form to the formlessness of
Being, while remaining scrupulously honest to his artistic
self.[16] His answer, in the following extract, is to attempt a
composition of decomposition and thus subvert the traditional conception of art as imposing order on reality:

Perhaps it's a dream, all a dream, that would surprise me, I'll wake,
in the silence, and never sleep again, it will be I, or dream, dream
again, dream of silence, a dream silence, full of murmurs, I don't
know, that's all words, never wake, all words, there's nothing else,
you must go on, that's all I know . . . it will be I, you must go on, I
can't go on, you must go on, I'll go on, you must say words as long
as there are any, until they find me, until they say me, strange pain,
strange sin, you must go on, perhaps it's done already, perhaps
they have said me already, perhaps they have carried me to the
threshold of my story, that would surprise me, if it opens it will be
I, it will be the silence, where I am, I don't know, I'll never know,
in the silence you don't know, you must go on, I can't go on, I'll go
on.[17]

Yet Beckett cannot be accused of misrepresenting reality in
any of his characters since their grotesque and barren worlds
are in fact far less distorting than those in naturalist fiction.
The latter merely creates a series of artificial forms and
techniques, such as verisimilitude, which only violate a study
of man's trackless inner being. On the contrary, in his search
for a transparent language, he represents: 'an artist who
seems literally skewered on the ferocious dilemma of expression. Yet he continues to wriggle.'[18] This anguish of
helplessness is strikingly conveyed in the above passage. We
have no visual concrete details which normally keep the
imagination afloat and so the amorphous voice becomes a

torrent of word sounds, swept precipitant into our ears. Like a swollen cataract the passage rushes towards its own dissolution, eroding the chimeric promise of meaning, melting into pure rhythm and revolting against 'Grammar and Style!'.[19]

That does not however imply a relinquishing of formal control leading to chaos. The sounds of the hero are not cacophony but ordered, breathless dissonance. Unmoored to the visual, the language challenges our imagination not our memory and leads towards what Beckett has called: 'The most frightening of all human observations . . . when man faces himself, he is looking into the abyss.'[20] The protagonist lacks even the consolation of a fixed 'self' available for, or capable of, true self-reflection: 'It will be I, it will be the silence, where I am, I don't know . . . I can't go on, I'll go on.' The finality of those last words precludes alternatives and condemns him to unrelieved solitude, thus extending the poignant grotesquerie of his situation to nightmarish depths.

But we must not forget that only a meticulous attention to detail can yield such effects. And Beckett's genius manifests itself not only in the choice of words but also in their order and spacing, for instance, the simple strategy of weaving phrases together with a thread of differing pronouns so as to induce a sense of dark anonymity. Indeed much of the passage is arranged into patterns resembling those on a musical score. He thus orchestrates the flow of words with mathematical precision, combining elements of counterpoint and (less evidently) fugue, to create an aural vortex of controlled incoherency.[21]

Moreover, in his perverse way, this non-figure is extremely vulnerable, a representative of the excoriated sensibility of loss and loneliness. His baldachin proclaims 'Nothing is more real than nothing'[22], and it casts a critical shadow upon humanity's death grip on materialism. In fact, the implicit question within this extraordinarily *affective* passage is whether the cessation of suffering is not more unbearable than suffering itself. There is, however, no direct answer, just as there is no verbal response to Lear's plea: 'Who is it can tell me who I am?'[23] The greatest crime is feigned understanding and so we must silently watch the hero being gradually enveloped in the dispassionate flux of time. In short, this passage (the culmination of the *Trilogy*) is a dramatically non-dramatic response to an issue Beckett addressed early in his career:

Who will create an art that acknowledges the inaccessibility of the object, that admits chaos and in so doing 'fails', that grants the unavailability of ultimate answers? Who will take woe, want, absence, nothingness for his subject?[24]

Yet although the passage admits of woe and want there is finally an overriding feeling, at once harrowing and exhilarating, of courage and endurance. The hero's words echo intractability, a refusal to relinquish his tussle, and they breed a strange excitement and *feeling* for life, which vivifies our awareness of our reflective selves. But this is only possible if we abandon preconceptions and attempt to hear the words with our eyes and see the sounds with our ears, because 'When the sense is sleep the words go to sleep . . . When the sense is dancing, the words dance.'[25]

The succinct redundancy of the dramatic dialogues in *Endgame* is in stark contrast to the logorrhea of *The Unnamable* passage, and in part derives from the exigencies of the stage, which demands attention to spectacle, gesture and audience. Yet Beckett welcomed the discipline drama imposed since it acted as both a curb and comfort, less encumbering than the lawless region of fiction.[26] It also provided a way out of the creative impasse he had reached in *Nouvelles et Textes Pour Rien*.[27] Moreover, its inherent restrictions have paradoxically increased the range and flexibility of his expression. This is evident in Hamm and Clov's speeches below, in which we find greater rhythmic variation and more abrupt shifts in pace, tone and mood. Beckett is also more selective and subtle in his use of repetition so that it goes beyond mere intensification and can be employed, for example, in the refrain-like patterns of internal dialogue, to create a sense of quiescence and even stasis. Or it can be a means of deliberately undermining the linear progression of thought and so forcing us to become more conscious of our presence at a spectacle. He thus invites a more complete kind of sharing and participation in the artist's perception of a changing self than was possible in the fiction.

Hamm's speech gives us ample opportunities to discover the new demands Beckett makes in drama:

HAMM The end is in the beginning | and yet you go on.
(Pause)
Perhaps I could go on with my story, end it | and begin another.
(Pause)
Perhaps I could throw myself out on the floor.
(He pushes himself painfully off his seat, falls back again)
Dig my nails into the cracks | and drag myself forward with my fingers.
(Pause)
It will be the end | and there I'll be, wondering what can have brought it on | and wondering what can have . . .
(He hesitates)
. . . why it was so long coming.
(Pause)
There I'll be, in the old refuge, alone against the silence | and . . .
(He hesitates)
. . . the stillness.
If I can hold my peace, and sit quiet, it will be all over | with sound, and motion, all over | and done with.
(Pause)
I'll have called my father | and I'll have called my . . .
(He hesitates)
. . . my son. And even | twice, or three times, in case they shouldn't have heard me, the first time, or the second.
(Pause)
I'll say to myself, He'll come back.
(Pause)
And then?
(Pause)
And then?
(Pause)
He couldn't, he has gone too far.
(Pause)
And then?
(Pause. Very agitated)

All kinds of fantasies! That I'm being watched: A rat!
Steps! Breath held | and then . . .
(He breathes out)
Then babble, babble, words, like the solitary child who
turns himself into children, two, three, so as to be
together, and whisper together in the dark.
(Pause)
Moment upon moment, pattering down, like the millet
grains of . . .
(He hesitates)
. . . That old Greek, and all life long you wait for that to
mount up to a life.
(Pause) (He opens his mouth to continue, renounces)
Ah | let's get it over![28]

Here the extremely hushed, *largo* cadence of his words
requires initially an equally tranquil and reposed state in our
minds. This is evident in the calm and motionless opening
line which harbours a sense of unutterable solitude, of a mind
quietly oblivious to human companionship. It is followed in
the second line by a voice drily mocking the dreary persistence of moving from arbitrary beginnings to ephemeral
ends. But the faint glimmers of humour are soon replaced by
an immense penumbra of resignation hovering over the two
sentences and only deepened by the ironic 'perhaps'. Continuation appears hopeless, but more than that, the spectre of
'Time' as the unmoved mover is a harbinger of greater fears
and inexplicable mental paralysis.

The first hint of fear and first tinge of madness can be sifted
from the hushed 'floor' of the third line, it smells of
desperation. The scent of fear dissipates somewhat in the
following line to be replaced by a surge of underlying feeling
in the sequence of alliteration. The 'dig, drag, fingers' are all
spaced at nearly equal intervals and convey the measured
progression of a tortured mind, having to force taut and
knotted thoughts from the intellect into the still air. The
voice is clenched and raw, almost croaking with despair but
the sobs, more implied than heard, are under control. Then
the tone shifts and the next line harbours an odd, almost
visionary air in the whispered 'end', and with the semantic

support of 'wondering', it points towards Hamm's retreat from the present to a semi-hallucinatory state. This is as much in the past as in the future, since the phrase 'wondering what can have' is ambiguous: it can either be a projection of his future expectations or a return to an incident from the past.

Beckett himself has said there exists in *Endgame* a 'power of the text to claw, more inhuman than *Waiting for Godot*'.[29] This is made manifest in Hamm's speech when he repeatedly raises his hopes only to have them dashed, and the effect is intensified by our recognition of its inevitability. He is a victim of memories, which only momentarily and teasingly offer respite. For instance, the line ending in 'all over | and done with', appears to promise finality and certitude in its emphatic 'done'. But its implications are soon shattered in the succeeding line which ends in a half-choked sob. Then Hamm collects himself as if having a premonition of the ordeal ahead. The first 'And then?' is posed timidly and quite innocent of emotion but the impassive tone is suddenly broken by the second 'And then?', now totally transformed with a hissing kind of fright. Then Beckett carefully builds towards the third groping plea which is fraught with the horror of a broken spirit ruled by directionless dread. The apex of tension is reached in a flood of quivering images, 'A rat! Steps!', each revealed in a violent whisper, as if fearful of awakening more forbidden memories. (Needless to say the exclamation marks in the text hardly do justice to this aural portrait of imagined horrors and psychic nakedness.) Finally the tremulous, 'Then babble, babble, words, . . . in the dark' softens the nearly inhuman pitch of hysteria which the preceding words border upon.

This section illustrates that the more limited the fund of data in the language the more a potential resonance of meaning is maintained. Yet this mecca of unrealized meaning and association can only be appreciated by a developed sensibility, which to a large degree is based upon an abnegation of the intellect. It is evident for example, in the antepenultimate and penultimate lines of the passage, where the causal relation between Democritus' atomic theory and Zeno's paradox is superseded by the blistered and reviling tone of 'that old Greek', so that the cracked, carbuncular voice conjures a picture of acid spilled on an open wound, a wound emblematic of generosity and forgiveness. But even ignoring the moral implications, we find the voice of Hamm contracting our vision and intensifying the focus of our imaginative energies on his intolerable, self-absorbed condition. The language so simply phrased is converted into an expression of feverish frustration and its object is unfathomable. It is directed to nothing other than existence and the final line opening with the terrible sigh of, ' Ah', symbolizes a moan speaking to everyone and everything. Yet when the last four words, struggling to emerge and announce their meaning, finally issue gutturally from the constricted deeps of his throat, they retain a strength and resistance of willed anger implicitly gesturing to the *deus absconditus*.

Although the semantic content of the passage appears to contradict that observation and supplant 'implicitly' with 'impotently', after a closer reading the clenched utterance smacks more of resolution borne on a wave of indefatigable emotion. Beckett's method of composition sustains this conclusion, since the passage as a whole represents the kind of impressionism he observed at work in Proust, what he called: 'a non-logical statement of phenomena in the order and exactitude of their perception, before they have been distorted into intelligibility in order to be forced into a chain of cause and effect'.[30] This absence of logical relations allows the muffled suffering to leap from the words and animate feelings which open 'a window on the real'.[31] Thus Hamm, who forsakes habit and its handmaiden boredom, because his involuntary memory never sleeps, remains accessible to the jungle of feeling; so that what we extract from the gnarled, curdled language is the sensation of an invigorating plunge into 'the cruelties and enchantments of reality'.[32] The 'fantasies' may be more cruel than enchanting but his stubborn resistance, his refusal to succumb and retreat from pain is finally an affirmation of life and beckons us to do the same.

The logic of Clov's speech exists in a less tenuous state of intelligibility than that of Hamm's – instead its power derives from understatement. The sense of solitude is also more complete since a placid and somewhat ethereal tone informs the passage.

CLOV   They said to me, That's friendship, yes, yes, no question | you've found it. They said to me, Here's the place, stop, raise your head and look at all that beauty. That order! They said to me, Come now, you're not a brute beast, think upon these things and you'll see how all becomes clear . . . And simple! They said to me, What skilled attention they get, all these dying of their wounds.
(Pause)
I say to myself – sometimes, Clov, you must learn to suffer better than that | if you want them to weary of punishing you – one day. I say to myself sometimes, Clov, you must be there better than that | if you want them to let you go – one day. But I feel too old, and too far, to form new habits. Good, it'll never end, I'll never go.
Then one day suddenly, it ends, it changes, I don't understand, it dies, or it's me, I don't understand that either. I ask the words that remain – sleeping, waking, morning, evening. They have nothing to say.
(Pause)
I open the door of the cell | and go. I am so bowed I only see my feet, if I open my eyes, and between my legs | a little trail | of black dust. I say to myself | that the earth is extinguished, though I never saw it lit.
(Pause)
It's easy going.
(Pause)
When I drop | I'll weep | for happiness.[33]

The steady even cadence of Clov's half-whispering voice is sustained throughout the passage. The words fall limply and delicately from his tongue, yet are so completely composed as to create an uncanny distance between sound and source. Thus there is an eerie rift between speech and character so that the words as an expression of feeling, lack individuality: they are freed from the spokesman and allowed to take on a wider, more universal resonance. And whereas the localized voice of Hamm suggested remorseless, devouring time, this voice accepts the infinity of time and space with droning equanimity: 'Good, it'll never end, I'll never go'. But obviously Clov's assumed placidity, both masks and heightens an intense irony that pulsates within the words. The opening lines for example, 'They said to me, That's friendship, yes, yes, no question . . . And simple!' are a clear illustration of this. However once the words have *settled*, the irony is superseded by a sense of profound and simple resignation, and it recalls an observation made in the *Proust* essay about the impossibility of friendship, since 'it is the negation of that irremediable solitude to which every human being is condemned'.[34]

Yet Clov's disembodied voice and its bubbling font of understatement in the opening lines, palliates the stinging truth of the above comment and diverts attention from himself to the issue of man's illusory quest for knowledge and coherent order. The full absurdity of this inane adherence to fixed definitions and apodictic truths is revealed in the delicious pun on 'order' (that is to say, ordure) and magnified by the ironical increments of 'clear . . . And simple!' in the following line. The irony is blatantly parasitical but it in no way detracts from his implied belief that the only tenable position is a kind of amused detachment.

Clov communicates these feelings in seemingly rational sentences – his voice frail, vacant and featureless with the landscape of inflexion and accent stripped almost naked. However the straightforward and terse logic of the lines is inverted by his flat tones, so as to spark a sense of the irrational, in which the unconscious mind perceives dissociated phenomena. The faceless 'They', who are 'dying of their wounds', quietly echo this kind of limbo. His solitary world is peopled with vague allusions to another life, the life of sensible reality, and he hangs suspended in his universe, 'too old, and too far' – unable to recover an understanding of, or retain contact with 'them'. Yet there is no evident gloom and despondency in the voice since it is too objective (ostensibly) to be moved by intense passion. Nevertheless hard contactual logic is undermined in the line, 'Then one day suddenly, it ends, . . . I don't understand that either' and thus we are reminded 'of Schopenhauer's definition of the artistic procedure as "the contemplation of the world independently of reason".'[35] But more importantly, the plodding gravity of 'sleeping, waking, morning, evening', which follow hard upon the enigmatic 'it', reveal the rigidity and artifice of man's whole constructed world in which cyclic tedium can blanket knowledge, rendering it indistinct and obscure, so that '*They* have nothing to say', or conversely, *Ubi nihil vales, ibi nihil velis.*[36]

The theme of man's absurd intellectual quest is superseded in the following section by a quiet declivity towards an indefinable and ineradicable pathos, beginning with 'dying of their wounds' and reaching its nadir in the slow, steady shuffle forward from, 'if I open my eyes' to, 'a little trail | of black dust' which marks a rejection of man's spirit of inquiry. Thus, rather than confront the vicissitudes of life, Clov turns to particulars, and the hushed tone of 'black dust' conveys his absorption in a brighter, more primary reality of the self, which cries for a life beyond the intellect.[37] It is a feeling transmitted both through and from behind the words, when the proliferation of sibilance in the second half of the passage – so consonant with Clov's withdrawal – seems to all gather in the final word and rush forth from 'happiness' into an impersonal void. This word, the most emphatic in the passage, expresses a final purgation without the rough trappings of sentimentality. Indeed none of his characters exhibit a trace of self-pity, since they are all inherently sceptical creatures. In other words, 'the danger is in the neatness of identification.'[38] Or to use Kantian terms, there is always a necessary barrier between a pure form of subjective intuition and an object of experience. Thus we can never know the intrinsic self or *noumena* of another.[39] It is a reciprocal dilemma that neither the characters in their fictional worlds, nor we as observers, can ever resolve.

Among the various *portraits* assembled here, we find endless oppositions and contradictions, all of which oscillate on the fulcrum of Beckett's resounding 'perhaps'. As a consequence, none of his characters can be tragic heroes: they lack noble ideals and question if not destroy all shibboleths and icons. And although each has different shadings of pain, much like chiaroscuro on canvas, they lack aspirations, which again precludes tragic sublimity. However these heroes (heroes as a result of their unflinching honesty) are impregnated with a powerful sense of affirmation. Their continued existence is in itself a positive assertion. Or more fundamentally, the artist denies negation in the act of creating something from nothing. Genuine art is not capable of negation, absolute negation.

One critic inverts this argument to say that within Beckett's fictional universe 'the flashes of humour that light it up from time to time, serve only to intensify the settled sense of gloom and doom'.[40] He appears to conclude that the exfoliation of despair precludes genuine tenderness, whereas the reading indubitably proves otherwise. Admittedly, the ineluctable quandary facing all the characters in differing degrees is boredom, but they continually deflect its enervating effects with anger or humour. Pascal gives a very precise summary of their dilemma:

Rien n'est si insuportable a l'homme que d'etre dans un plein repos, sans passions, sans affaire, sans divertissement, sans application. Il sent alors son neant, son abandon, son insuffisance, sa dependance, son impuissance, son vide. Incontinent, il sortira du fond de son ame l'ennui, la noirceur, la tristesse, le chagrin, le depit, le desespoir.[41]

However Pascal's judgement cannot account for the extraordinary pangs Beckett provokes in us, or how the characters' words continue to ring in our ears. Part of the answer is found in the author's scrupulous regard for variation in rhythm, tone and tempo, so that each passage evinces a tender, almost caressing fidelity to the fusion of sound and sense, which in turn enhances the display of an internal labyrinth of moods. And at times this precise verbal carpentry entrances and mesmerizes our sensibility, producing an uncanny feeling that the characters have an autonomous existence outside the text. In essence therefore, they are the creations of a poet, if poetry is defined as a structure in which the form is equally as important as, and organically coincides with, the content, so as to generate a complex interrelationship between sound, sight and semantics. This in turn continues to provoke and compound our sense of the ineffable, so that there is, finally, only the constant and familiar echo of 'perhaps'. Although it is not a very sound lever for uncovering his appeal, we can venture to suggest that each of the passages is diffused with a light of rare compassion and with slightly more assurance, say that Beckett's view of life is one 'which seeks a meaning and a purpose beyond the physical needs of specific time and place'[42] and beckons us towards a tantalizing, unembraceable reality:

> peering out of my deadlight looking for another
> wandering like me eddying far from all the living
> in a convulsive space
> among the voices voiceless
> that throng my hiddenness.[43]

1. See Ludovic Janvier, *Samuel Beckett: par lui-même* (Paris, 1969), p. 181 and p. 161 respectively. Translated as follows: 'Man speaks only in so much as he is responding to language, while listening to what it is saying to him.' 'The human being is a singing creature who unites music and thought.'
2. It may be helpful, when considering Beckett's prose, to recall Aquinas' axiom 'Nihil in intellectu quod non prius in sensu.' Translation: 'Nothing is in the understanding which was not previously in the senses.' Beckett quotes the Italian version in his 'Dante . . . Bruno. Vico . . . Joyce' essay in Samuel Beckett, Marcel Brion, *et al.*, *Our Exagmination Round His Factification for Incamination of Work in Progress* (Paris, 1929), p. 10, 'niente à nell' intelleto che prima non sia nel senso'. Equally useful are some comments from Charles Olsen's essay on 'Projective Verse' in *Selected Writings*, edited by R. Creeley (New York, 1966), pp. 17–18, p. 26. They may suggest fresh criteria for judging Beckett's *prose*: 'that verse will only do in which a poet manages to register both the acquisitions of his ear *and* the pressures of his breath . . . It is by their syllables that words juxtose in beauty, by these particles of sound as clearly as by the sense of words which they compose. In any

given instance, because there is a choice of words, the choice if a man is in there, will be, spontaneously the obedience of his ear to the syllables. The fineness and the practice, lie here, at the minimum and source of speech . . . down through the workings of his own throat to that place where breath comes from, where breath has its beginnings, where drama has to come from, where, the coincidence is, all act springs.'

3. Alec Reid, *All I Can Manage More Than I Could* (Dublin, 1969), p. 33. Reid quotes from Beckett's letter to Alan Schneider, 12 August 1957.

4. Recording: *MacGowran Speaking Beckett*, Claddagh Records Ltd. (Dublin, 1969). Limitations of length have prevented my including a completely representative selection of passages from the recording.

5. Beckett, 'Dante . . . Joyce', p. 15.

6. Samuel Beckett, 'Dante . . . Joyce', p. 14. This statement by Beckett refers to Joyce's language and it ends with the comment that: 'His writing is not *about* something; *it is that something itself*'. Again this could equally be a description of Beckett's prose.

7. Alan Schneider, 'Waiting for Beckett', in John Calder *et al.*, *Beckett at 60. A Festschrift* (London, 1967), p. 34.

8. J. Boehme, *Mysterium Magnum*, translated by J. Sparrow and edited by C. J. Barker (London, 1924), vol. 1, part 2, chapter 35, section 57, p. 352. 'Now whosoever hath the understanding of the senses, viz. of the spirits of the letters, so that he doth understand how the senses are set or compounded in the *lubet*, he understands it in the framing of the word, when the same is formed or brought forth to substance; and is able to understand the *sensual* (natural or essential) language of the whole creation.'

9. Gabriel d'Aubarède, interview in *Nouvelles Littéraires*, 16 Feb. 1961, quoted by Ludovic Janvier, *Pour Samuel Beckett* (Paris, 1966), pp. 43–4. Translation: 'I conceived *Molloy* and the others the day I became conscious of my folly. Only then did I begin to write the things I feel.' As a complement to Beckett's statement we might consider Michel Foucault's quotation from Destutt de Tracy's 'Éléments d'Idéologie', 1, p. 35, in *Les Mots et les Choses* (Paris, 1966), p. 254: 'Penser, comme vous voyez, *c'est toujours sentir*, et ce n'est rien que sentir.' Translation: 'To think as you see *is always to feel* and is nothing other than to feel.'

10. Paul Valéry, 'Préface aux Carnet de Léonard de Vinci' p. 211, in Jacob Hytier, *La Poétique de Valéry* (Paris, 1970), p. 29. Translation: 'To restore by means of conscious operations the

value of sensuality and the emotional power of things', which Valéry defined as the goal of art. Again Foucault provides useful parallels in *Les Mots et les Choses*, p. 133, when he speaks of, 'Le grande utopie d'un langage parfaitment transparent où les choses elles-mêmes seraient nommées sans brouillage, . . . par un langage si naturel qu'il traduirait la pensée comme le visage quand il exprime une passion.' Translation: 'The great utopia of a perfectly transparent language in which things themselves could be named without a fog of confusion . . . by a language so natural that it would translate thought like a face when it is expressing a passion.'

11. Samuel Beckett, and Georges Duthuit, *Proust and Three Dialogues* (London, 1965), p. 64, pp. 65–6.

12. Samuel Beckett, 'Hommage à Jack B. Yeats', in *Les Lettres Nouvelles*, no. 14, April 1954, p. 619. Translation: 'The artist who risks his whole being comes from nowhere and he has no friends.'

13. Hugh Kenner, *Samuel Beckett: A Critical Study* (London, 1962), p. 91.

14. Samuel Beckett, *Malone Dies* (London, 1968), pp. 5–6. Stress marks (for syllabic divisions) and pause marks (long vertical strokes) are my own in this and subsequent passages. These markings may not be sufficiently complex for a linguistics scholar but on the other hand a sophisticated system of notation would be self-defeatingly intricate.

15. L. E. Harvey, *Samuel Beckett: Poet and Critic* (Princeton, 1970), p. 194.

16. Edmund Husserl, *The Phenomenology of Internal Time–Consciousness*. Edited by M. Heidegger, translated by J. S. Churchill (London, 1966), p. 100. Husserl's statement below, if considered in context, clarifies my use of that ambiguous term 'Being': 'We can only say that this flux is something which we name in conformity with what is constituted, but it is nothing temporally *Objective*. It is the absolute subjectivity and has the absolute properties of something to be denoted metaphorically as *flux*, as a point of actuality, primal source point, that from which springs the now, and so on. In the lived experience of actuality we have the primal source-point and a continuity of moments of reverberation'.

17. Samuel Beckett, *The Unnamable* (London, 1973), p. 418.

18. Beckett, and Duthuit, *Proust*, p. 110.

19. Harvey, *Samuel Beckett: Poet and Critic*, p. 434. Quoted from Beckett's letter to Axel Kaun. Beckett also comments on the *disciplina* of language which appear 'to have become just as obsolete as a Biedermeier bathing suit or the imperturbability

of a gentleman. A mask'.

20. J. Gruen, 'Samuel Beckett talks about Beckett', an interview in *Vogue* Feb. 1970, p. 108.

21. Marcel Mihalovici, 'My Collaboration with Samuel Beckett', in Calder *et al*. *Beckett at 60*, pp. 20–1. Mihalovici attests to Beckett's musical ability in work together on an opera libretto: 'Beckett's help was, I can say, essential at that point. Because Beckett is a remarkable musician – did you know it? He possesses an astonishing musical intuition'.

22. Axiom attributed to Democritus of Abdera.

23. *King Lear*, I. iv. 238, Arden Shakespeare, edited by K. Muir (London, 1971), p. 48.

24. Harvey, *Samuel Beckett: Poet and Critic*, p. 400.

25. Beckett, 'Dante . . . Joyce', p. 14.

26. Reid, *All I Can Manage*, p. 20.

27. In a 'Letter to Jerome Lindon' 10 April 1951, from Calder *et al*. *Beckett at 60*, p. 19. Beckett describes the difficulties he was having with *Textes pour Rien*, 'I do not know if it will be able to make a book. It will perhaps be a time for nothing.'

28. Samuel Beckett, *Endgame* (New York, 1958), pp. 69–70.

29. Patrick Murray, *The Tragic Comedian: A Study of Samuel Beckett* (Cork, 1970), p. 58.

30. Beckett and Duthuit, *Proust*, p. 86.

31. *Ibid*., p. 28.

32. *Ibid*., p. 22.

33. Beckett, *Endgame*, pp. 80–1.

34. Beckett and Duthuit, *Proust*, p. 63. In order to amplify and clarify this statement we should turn to a preceding quote by Proust which he cites: 'One desires to be understood because one desires to be loved, and one desires to be loved because one loves. We are indifferent to the understanding of others, and their love is an importunity.'

35. *Ibid*., p. 87.

36. Arnold Geulincx's axiom – translation: 'You may want nothing where you can do nothing' aptly summarizes the corresponding folly of attaching value to the external body.

37. Harvey, *Samuel Beckett: Poet and Critic*, p. 204. Harvey observes that: 'Quite often he is overtaken by a profound unreality of the self called Sam Beckett who goes through the motions of day to day living, mechanically and without conviction.'

38. Beckett, 'Dante . . . Joyce', p. 3.

39. Immanuel Kant, *Critique of Pure Reason*, Translated by F. Max Muller. (New York, 1961). See pp. 166–72 for a full discussion. Beckett arrives at a similar conclusion, in *Proust*, p. 58.

'We imagine that the object of our desire is a being that can be laid down before us, enclosed within a body. Alas! it is the extension of that being to all the points of space and time that it has occupied and will occupy. If we do not possess contact with such a place and with such an hour we do not possess that being. But we cannot touch all these points.'

40. Murray, *The Tragic Comedian*, p. 42.
41. Blaise Pascal, 'Ennui et qualités essentielles de l'homme', in *Pensées* edited by Louis Lafuma (Paris, 1952), p. 147. Translation: 'Nothing is more intolerable to man than a state of complete repose without passions, without business, without amusement, without occupation. It is then he feels his nothingness, his inadequacy, his dependence, his emptiness. And immediately there will rise from the depths of his soul, weariness, gloom, misery, chagrin, vexation, despair.'
42. Ihab Hassan, 'The Literature of Silence: From Henry Miller to Beckett and Burroughs', *Encounter*, vol. 28, January 1967, p. 80.
43. Samuel Beckett, *Collected Poems in English and French* (London, 1977), p. 59.

'Early Modern Ireland, 1534–1691': a re-assessment

M. A. G. Ó TUATHAIGH

Some forty years ago there began a new era in Irish historical writing, as research took the place of rhetoric, and dispassionate enquiry and exposition replaced what had too often been highly passionate assertion and polemic. Some of the pioneers of that flowering of historical scholarship are now in the twilight of distinguished academic careers, for example, T. W. Moody and R. Dudley Edwards. Sadly, some others have already passed on. Among these was Gerard A. Hayes–McCoy, one of whose last contributions to Irish historical writing is contained in the volume under review.[1] The fruits of their labours, in their own writings and in the writings of the many historians whom they trained, are a lasting testimony to their influence. In many ways, also, this *New History of Ireland* (hereinafter *NHI*) may stand as a reference for the progress of Irish historical scholarship from the early 1930s to the early 1970s. In a very special way the *NHI* will be associated with T. W. Moody, the senior of the three editors: it was he who first saw the angel in marble, and together with his fellow editors he has worked hard to bring it to completion. Indeed, though it can hardly have been by choice, it is probably fitting that the first volume to be published (out of sequence) covers the early modern period, from the reformation to the Williamite victory and the consolidation of the protestant ascendancy. This, after all, was the period which first attracted the critical attention of Moody and his fellow pioneers of the 1930s.

The project, conceived on a grand scale and published under the auspices of the Royal Irish Academy, is organized in the manner of the *New Cambridge Modern History*, with individual specialists providing chapters in a volume covering a recognized chronological span. This format calls for strong editorial control, if the reader is to be favoured with a coherent narrative, and if unnecessary repetition is to be avoided. In general this volume does indeed benefit from tight editorial control. Overlapping is kept to a minimum, and while some of the seams between consecutive chapters might have been better masked, there are no serious gaps in the main narrative. The backbone, or 'primary narrative' of the volume is mainly concerned with political, constitutional and administrative developments in Ireland during this 'age of disruption'. In addition to this primary narrative there are three 'panorama' chapters (for 1534 by D. B. Quinn and K. W. Nicholls, for *c.* 1600 by R. A. Butlin, and for *c.* 1685 by J. H. Andrews); two chapters on the Irish economy (with A. Clarke covering the period 1600–60 and L. M. Cullen dealing with 1660–91); a solid chapter on Irish coinage 1534–1691 by Michael Dolley; and four chapters on what may be described as intellectual history – the Irish language in the early modern period, by Brian Ó Cuív; the English language in the same period, by Alan Bliss; Irish literature in Latin, by Benignus Millett; and the Irish abroad, by John J. Silke. These last four chapters are, however, relegated to the end of the volume, where their collective impact on the main narrative is not as significant as it ought to be. The volume opens with an introduction from T. W. Moody and concludes with a most useful bibliography by J. G. Simms.

The allocation of space to the different chronological sections is somewhat uneven, though in this it probably reflects the uneven state of knowledge and research within the early modern period. The treatment of the seventeenth century is thus considerably more detailed and, in many ways, more nuanced than that of the sixteenth century. In fact, the primary narrative for the period 1534–1603 was provided by one contributor, the late G. A. Hayes–McCoy. Here the narrative style is characteristically lucid and lively. The narrative is good on political and military history, and has a sharper interpretative edge for the later sixteenth century than for the earlier period. The chapter lacks a comparative dimension, however, and it is a pity that the author was unable to take advantage of more recent work on the period, notably by Bradshaw, Ellis and Canny.[2] There is some compensation for the lacunae in Hayes–McCoy's account in the '1534 panorama' by Quinn and Nicholls. Remarkably clear and coherent in its presentation, this survey also points out honestly the gaps and uncertainties in the present state of knowledge of sixteenth-century Ireland, and often sets out, albeit obliquely, a challenging agenda for future work, for instance, the lack of information on the actual religious practices and customs of the people, as distinct from the more formal story of ecclesiastical institutions. Here the work of John Bossy suggests some of the questions which remain to be asked of religious life in early modern Ireland.[3]

In his introductory essay T. W. Moody seeks to set out in broad strokes the main themes of the volume, the matrix of events which gives its internal coherence to this period. Thus, we find analysis of the revolution in government which saw a centralized state on the English model gradually, and not without resistance, replace the rather loosely decentralized Gaelic, and indeed Norman–Gaelic structures of the late medieval period; the long and uneven revolution in land ownership, which saw first the Gaelic lords and later, after religion had become the crucial cleavage in determining every form of power, the entire Catholic landowning class dispossessed and replaced by a Protestant landowning class holding title under English law and custom. In addition to this revolution in land ownership, these centuries also witnessed several attempts at plantation, that is to say, the introduction of a substantial number of planters (as modest landowners or as tenants), and the inevitable displacement or depression of existing owners and occupiers. The story of Irish plantations of the sixteenth and seventeenth centuries is one of extraordinary complexity, and several chapters in this volume (particularly those on the economy and the survey chapters by the geographers, Andrews and Butlin) very properly stress the difficulties involved in making generaliza-

tions on, for example, the impact of planters in various parts
of the country on economic activity and social life. It is
undeniably true, of course, that the most successful attempt
at plantation (successful, that is, in terms of the impact and
permanence of settlement) was the planter society settled in
successive waves in Ulster during the seventeenth century.
The legacy of this plantation remains to this day a major
problem not merely in the maintenance of peace and order
within Ireland, but also in the context of Anglo-Irish relations. Yet, even here caution is required in estimating the
immediate impact of the early planters on the host society. In
the economic sphere, for example, Aiden Clarke, writing of
the early seventeenth century, concludes that: 'In general, it
seems clear that while the resources of the province were
exploited more intensively in the seventeenth century than
they had been in the past, the manner in which they were
exploited was not markedly different. What the plantation
altered in Ulster was not the economy, but control over the
economy' (p. 177). Several contributors stress the need for a
careful differentiation between various groups of planters,
pointing out that their intellectual no less than their material
provenance was a key factor in determining their impact on
and adaptability to conditions in the brave new world in
Ireland. Notwithstanding this sound advice, the volume is
rather short on information about the settlers. In fact, in
discussing and analysing the various themes set out in his
introduction by T. W. Moody, the *NHI* scores highly in
elucidating what, to borrow from Robinson and Gallagher,
may be described as 'the official mind' of early modern
British colonialism. The general assumptions of official
policy, the general context (not merely British but also
European) in which such policy was formulated and im-
plemented, and the main political consequences of these
policies, are all well handled by the contributors. As mentioned, the detail is greater for the seventeenth century where
Clarke, Corish and Simms were all drawing on considerable
resources of scholarly work produced, for the most part, by
themselves. However, one would have wished for a more

detailed look at the attitudes and prejudices, the talents, habits and convictions of the settlers themselves. Of crucial importance is the responsiveness of the settlers to, on the one hand, the dictates of official policy, and on the other hand, to the actuality of their situation as planters in a strange and often hostile land. In fairness, it must be said that on these very questions the reader can probably infer quite an amount of useful data from the chapters on economic and social life, but a more formal treatment of attitudes and perceptions among the planters would have enhanced the volume.

If the attitudes of the colonists have often to be searched out or inferred, the attitudes of the Gaelic Irish, indeed the full cultural matrix which was almost destroyed in the 'age of disruption', are aspects of the story on which the *NHI* is, quite frankly, disappointing. This indeed is rather a pity. The ramifications and full resonance of the kulturkampf of early modern Ireland are virtually impossible to comprehend if the 'world-view' of one party in the struggle remains largely unexplored. Several of the contributors advert to the Gaelic dimension of their themes (the Quinn and Nicholls survey does rather more than this), and make brief sorties into the Gaelic source material. But these sorties are too brief, and there seems to be a general sharing of Hayes–McCoy's assumption that 'the surviving evidence permits but slight insight into any Gaelic Irishman's mind' (p. 116). This seems something of an exaggeration when we turn to Brian Ó Cuív's extended bibliographical essay on Gaelic literature, and indeed on Gaelic writing in general for this period. Here we have an abundance of source material which cries out for interpretation; material which, if used sensitively by those linguistically equipped, would yield rather more than a slight insight into the minds of at least certain categories of Gaelic Irishmen during the sixteenth and seventeenth centuries. Indeed, the chapters by Ó Cuív, Alan Bliss (a brief but suggestive essay on the English dialect in Ireland), Benignus Millett (Irish literature in Latin), and John Silke (the Irish abroad) together constitute the raw materials for a history of intellectual life, of beliefs and attitudes, principles and aspirations of various groups involved in the cultural conflict of the period. The work of interpretation remains to be done, and the *NHI* suffers from this fact.

Let us take a few examples from this Gaelic material. Two of the most interesting Gaelic writers of the early seventeenth century, Seathrún Céitinn and Pádraigín Haicéad, were of Old-English rather than of Gaelic stock (and there are other examples of this also), a fact which prompts certain questions on the process of cultural integration in late medieval Ireland. More significant still is the fact that some of the more explicitly, indeed aggressively, political poetry of the early seventeenth century (e.g. 'Mo thruaighe mar tá Éire', 'Eirghe mo dhúithche le Dia', 'Muscail do mhisneach, a Bhanbha'), was written by poets who at one time or other were in exile in Catholic Europe. It is true, of course, that from the late sixteenth century at least some poets from the traditional bardic families (e.g. Tadhg Dall Ó Huiginn and Fear Flatha Ó Gnímh) had begun to write of the cultural and political turmoil which was all around them. Many poets of the traditional order, however, remained wedded to seemingly irrelevant material, such as clever linguistic games, oblivious to the seismic changes taking place in the Ireland of their day. Indeed, so hopelessly out of touch with political reality did they seem, that the exiled Archbishop of Tuam (Flaithrí Ó Maoilchonaire) chided them as 'coin iad go n-iomad feasa/ Ag gleich fán easair fhalaimh', that is to say, 'hounds of great knowledge wrangling over an empty dish' (p. 539). Of course, the conservatism of the bardic class is intelligible within the institutional and social structure of Gaelic Ireland. The real focus of interest, however, ought to be the provenance and personnel, the timing and motivation of *innovation* in late sixteenth- and early seventeenth-century Gaelic poetry.

Even a short discussion of some of the more accessible of Ó Cuív's sources suggests that there may be a prima facie case for saying that the politicization of cultural consciousness was greatly intensified (and given a decidedly religious tone) by the aggressive counter–Reformation spirit which

Irish poets and clerics in exile encountered in Catholic Europe. Nor is it Gaelic poetry alone which raises such intellectual questions. For example, the innovatory aspects of Céitinn's history of Ireland, *Foras Feasa ar Éirinn*, suggests that there may have been something involved here of what Peter Burke has called 'the sense of history' which had its origins in the Renaissance. How far, we may ask, does Céitinn's work satisfy Burke's criteria for this sense of history – 'the sense of anachronism', 'the awareness of evidence', and 'the interest in causation'.[4] This whole question of the impact of the Renaissance and Counter–Reformation on Irish intellectual life remains to be investigated. A reading of this volume of the *NHI* suggests that it is possible, if paradoxical, that the intellectual life of the Irish of this period was at its liveliest and most interesting among the exiles. That there was considerable richness and variety in this intellectual life is undeniable. As Benignus Millett reminds us: 'The Latin literature of the period under review was not exclusively ecclesiastical. It was also a literature of medical doctors, lawyers, university fellows, schoolmasters, poets and lexicographers' (p. 565).

There is little need to labour further the essential and obvious point that there is still a great deal of work to be done in making the existing source material yield up its full measure of information on the elements of conflict in early modern Ireland. It is surely not unreasonable to hope, indeed to expect, that an Irish historian of our generation may do for Gaelic Ireland what, for example, Nathan Wachtel has done for the conquered Peruvian Indian, particularly since Wachtel had to deal with material which was a great deal more problematic for the historian than are the existing Gaelic sources.[5]

To speak of what yet remains to be done is, of course, in no way to underestimate the achievement in historical understanding which this volume represents. The editors and contributors are themselves well aware of that remains to be done, as the lively and conflicting opinions and hypotheses on demographic patterns in this period clearly indicate.

Nevertheless, without the scholarly work contained in this impressive volume there would be no point in seeking to refine further issues of mind and motive. And, if historians of this generation feel able to ask about the early modern period questions which are new and different to the questions which concerned their predecessors, then this in itself is a striking tribute to the solid and scholarly foundations which are represented by this volume. Finally, let it be said that in all aspects of presentation this volume is a credit to its editors and to its publishers.

1. T. W. Moody, F. X. Martin and F. J. Byrne (eds.), *A New History of Ireland*, vol. 3, *Early Modern Ireland, 1534–1691* (Clarendon Press, Oxford, 1976).
2. See, for example, Brendan Bradshaw, 'Cromwellian Reform and the Origins of the Kildare Rebellion, 1533–34', *Transactions of the Royal Historical Society*, vol. 27, 1976, pp. 69–93; 'The Elizabethans and the Irish', *Studies*, vol. 66, 1977, pp. 38–50. S. G. Ellis, 'Tudor Policy and the Kildare Ascendancy in the Lordships of Ireland, 1496–1534', *Irish Historical Studies*, vol. 20, 1977, pp. 235–71; 'The Kildare Rebellion and the Early Henrician Reformation', *The Historical Journal*, vol. 19, no. 4, 1976, pp. 807–30. Nicholas P. Canny, *The Elizabethan Conquest of Ireland: A Pattern Established, 1565–76* (Hassocks, Sussex, 1976); 'The Permissive Frontier: the Problem of Social Control in English Settlements in Ireland and Virginia 1550–1650', in K. R. Andrews, N. P. Canny and P. Hair (eds.), *The Westward Enterprise* (Liverpool, 1978), pp. 17–44; 'Dominant Minorities: English Settlers in Ireland and Virginia, 1550–1650', in A. Hepburn (ed.), *Minorities in History* (London, 1978), pp. 51–69. See also the chapters by Brendan Bradshaw and Hugh Kearney in Brian Farrell (ed.), *The Irish Parliamentary Tradition* (Dublin, 1973).
3. John Bossy, *The English Catholic Community, 1570–1850* (London, 1975).
4. Peter Burke, *The Renaissance Sense of the Past* (London, 1969), p. 1.
5. Nathan Wachtel, *The Vision of the Vanquished: The Spanish Conquest of Peru through Indian Eyes* (Hassocks, Sussex, 1977).